THE DISCIPLING CYCLE SERIES

Becoming Christlike

Andy and Kim Harrison

LifeWay Press
Nashville, TN

ISBN 0-6330-0460-X

This book is the text for course number CG-0539 in the subject area "Personal Life-
Youth" of the Christian Growth Study Plan.

Dewey Decimal Classification: 248.83
Subject Heading: CHRISTIAN LIFE, TEENAGERS

Unless otherwise indicated, Scripture quotations are from the *New American
Standard Bible*, © Copyright The Lockman Foundation, 1960, 1962, 1963, 1968,
1971, 1972, 1973, 1975, 1977.
Used by permission.

Scripture quotations marked (NIV) are from the Holy Bible,
New International Version. Copyright © 1973, 1978, 1984 by International Bible Society.
Used by permission.

Printed in the United States of America.
To order additional copies of this resource: WRITE LifeWay Church Resources Customer Service,
127 Ninth Avenue, North, Nashville, TN 37234-0113; FAX order to (615) 251-5933;
PHONE 1-800-458-2772; EMAIL to CustomerService@lifeway.com;
or visit the LifeWay Christian Store serving you.

Art Direction & Designs: Edward Crawford

Youth Section
Discipleship and Family Group
LifeWay Christian Resources
Of the Southern Baptist Convention
127 Ninth Avenue, North
Nashville, TN 37234-0152

CONTENTS

THE AUTHORS

Andy Harrison serves as Student Ministry and Education Specialist for the Baptist General Convention of Oklahoma. He assists churches in Oklahoma with youth Sunday School and Discipleship. Andy is a graduate of Oklahoma Baptist University and attended Southwestern Baptist Theological Seminary.

Andy and Kim ministered together on staff in the local church for nearly two decades, and it was during that time they developed The Discipling Cycle for their own students.

The Harrisons strongly believe that the years of adolescence are crucial in grounding students in the Word of God and in the spiritual disciplines of the faith. It is their hope that the curriculum provided in The Discipling Cycle will encourage Biblical discipleship in the church.

This book is dedicated to their children, Ted, Caleb, and Victoria.

FOREWARD

Jesus has commanded in the Great Commission to "Therefore go and make disciples of all nations, baptizing them in the name of the Father and of the Son and of the Holy Spirit, and teaching them to obey everything I have commanded you . . ." (Matt. 28:19-20a emphasis mine). Youth ministries in our country today have often failed at this task, not because the kids are unwilling, but because we as leaders have under challenged them. I have found that youth respond to a challenge more deeply and with greater sacrifice than any age group I know. With this shared conviction, Andy & Kim Harrison have developed The Discipling Cycle.

This book is more than a series of Bible studies, it is a pattern and plan for the challenge of youth discipleship. From the commitment to prayer for adult leaders to the one-on-ones with students, The Discipling Cycle presents a Christlike model for discipling youth. The Bible studies themselves are deeper in focus than much of the youth curriculum published today and consistently confront the student with Christ Himself.

The Discipling Cycle is designed to use the Word of God, prayer, and the consistent love of a discipling leader to challenge good students to become godly ones; ones able to internalize *2 Timothy 2:2, "And the things you have heard me say in the presence of many witnesses entrust to reliable men who will also be qualified to teach others."*

This program ought to be in every church and I challenge you to challenge your students and watch them grow *"in wisdom and stature, and in favor with God and men."*

Henry T. Blackaby

INTRODUCTION

Welcome to *The Discipling Cycle Series*, a three-year course designed to help develop strong, biblical discipleship in your church. This book is titled *Becoming Christlike*, and is one of three books in this series. Each book represents 30 weeks of in-depth Bible study. The other two books are *Understanding and Knowing God* and *Seek, Share, Serve*. Each of these books also includes 30 weeks of study to help students become equipped in personal Bible study, Scripture memory, and practical life applications. *Understanding and Knowing God* focuses on deepening one's relationship with God and helping youth gain an accurate concept of Him. *Seek, Share, Serve* focuses on evangelism, outreach, and discipleship. A Leader's Guide is available for each resource.

BECOMING CHRISTLIKE: A GREAT PLACE TO BEGIN

Becoming Christlike is the book in *The Discipling Cycle Series* which guides the student in the area of godliness. Youth will be strengthened in personal disciplines and character qualities. This is an ideal place to begin the series. However, it is not necessary that you start *The Discipling Cycle Series* with any specific book in the series. It has not been developed with a "book one, book two, book three" approach. In fact, *Becoming Christlike* could be book one, two, or three, depending on where a student begins the cycle. You can begin *The Discipling Cycle Series* with any of the three workbooks in the series. The Bible study leader will find many helpful suggestions to facilitate this program in *Becoming Christlike Leader's Guide* (ISBN 0-6330-0461-8), also available at LifeWay Christian Stores or by calling 1-800-458-2772.

SCRIPTURE MEMORY

Scripture memory is an important aspect of *Becoming Christlike*, and a vital part of each week's journey. Without Scripture memory, a serious study of the Bible will be significantly impaired. As the believer memorizes the verses suggested in *Becoming Christlike*, he or she will see how the Holy Spirit uses the verses to hold the believer accountable to principles learned each week. These verses will help form a clear image of what the believer's life is supposed to look like.

The weekly verses in Becoming Christlike can be memorized by topic or title. Although the majority of Scripture memory topics are the same as the title of the study, some are different. Always use the topic found inside the Scripture Memory box on Day 1 of each study. Below is an example of how the verses will be listed each week.

SCRIPTURE MEMORY
The Believer's Life
■ 2 Corinthians 5:17
■ Galatians 2:20
■ Ephesians 4:24

In most of the studies you will find three verses in the Scripture Memory box, but you only need to choose and memorize one of the verses each week. When you have selected your verse for the week, write it on a card or piece of paper and place it somewhere you spend a lot of time.

This is the way you will want to memorize: topic to reference; reference to verse. When someone helps you review your verses, ask him or her to give you the topic, then you recite the Scripture reference and quote the verse.

Make use of idle minutes by reviewing your verses. Take your verses with you to school and ask someone in your class, a nonbeliever maybe, to test you on them when you have free time. Scripture memory is a challenge, but it can also be fun. And you will never look back and regret having done it! Make this a serious commitment. You will soon see that the rewards are grand compared to the little time and effort it takes to memorize Scripture. Decide now to make Scripture memory a priority.

DAILY BIBLE STUDY

In addition to the Scripture Memory box, each week includes five days of Bible study relating to that week's topic. It is set up this way to encourage daily Bible study. You will gain much more from a study in *The Discipling Cycle Series* when you approach it daily, rather than doing it all at once. Thirty weeks is a long haul. Determine now to make this a priority not only for week one, but for week nine, week 15, week 22, every week. And for those weeks when you fail, remember that you are not on a performance basis with God. It was not your works that saved you; it is not your works that keep you right before Him. Don't let guilt become your motivator, for it will not motivate. It will only tie you up in a noose. Learn to recognize the gentle prompting of the Holy Spirit. Don't work to please God, work because you already please God in Christ! Embrace this truth for yourself on the bad days as well as the good days.

The studies contain a variety of types of questions. Some will have obvious answers from the passage. Some will be personal and will require a more individual answer. Others will cause you to think and will not necessarily have one right answer. If you find that you do not understand a question, give the Holy Spirit some time to make it clear to you. It may be that you still do not receive an answer. Maybe He is not dealing with you in this particular area. If this happens, do not get discouraged, simply move on to the next question.

We are constantly amazed at the level of depth that students exhibit in answering questions in this study, and even more excited about how their actions reflect a true grasp of the principles. You have that same potential. Never let Satan convince you otherwise!

WEEK 1
THE NEW LIFE

DAY 1

For the next 30 weeks, you will study what it means to be like Christ in specific areas of your life, such as your attitude, behavior, and character. Jesus has purchased you. You are His. He has every right to claim you and to make claims on the way you live. His plan for you is to make you more like Himself. The following is a simple exercise to show you how this godliness or Christlikeness is a theme found throughout the Scriptures.

SCRIPTURE MEMORY
The Believer's Life
■ 2 Corinthians 5:17
■ Galatians 2:20
■ Ephesians 4:24

1. **Using the following Scripture references, fill in the blanks.**

    I am to be _____, and _____,
    because God in Christ _____ (Eph. 4:32).
    I am to _____, because Christ _____
    (Eph. 5:2).
    I am to be _____ because God _____ (Lev. 11:45).
    I am to be _____ because God _____ (Matt. 5:48).
    I am to _____ because God _____ (Luke 6:35-36).
    I am to _____, because God _____
    (1 John 4:11)

2. **From what you know about Jesus, why would you want to pattern your life after His?**

"The goal or standard toward which we are to strive is nothing less than that of a perfect Christian character. . .Christ Himself was the embodiment and revelation of what God would have man to be. To be like Christ is, therefore, the goal of the Christian's ambition."[1] —Walter T. Conner

Read 2 Corinthians 5:17.

3. **"Therefore, if any man is in Christ. . ." Who is the person who is "in Christ"? (John 3:3 may help here.)**

4. **How does 2 Corinthians 5:17 describe the person who is in Christ?**

5. **What do you think this means?**

> "It is not a question of a good man who died two thousand years ago. It is a living Man, still as much a man as you and still as much God as He was when He created the world, really coming and interfering with your very self; killing the old natural self in you and replacing it with the kind of self He has. At first, only for moments. Then for longer periods. Finally, if all goes well, turning you permanently into a different sort of thing; into a new little Christ, a being which, in its own small way, has the same kind of life as God; which shares in His power, joy, knowledge and eternity."[2] —C. S. Lewis

6. **What would make you suspicious that something was old, though it claimed to be new?**

7. **How does this relate to the new life of the Christian as described in today's verse?**

We are accustomed to thinking of "new" as something that can and will become old. But new life in Christ doesn't change. It doesn't become old. The new life is just as new today as when you asked Jesus to come into your life, and will be just as new tomorrow. We must not think of it as an old life that becomes new either. Salvation is transformation—an old life that is replaced with a new life. The old life is the sin nature. The new life is Christ's life in you! It is a transformed life.

Read Galatians 2:20.

8. **What does this verse say about the old life?**

9. **What does it say about the new life?**

"Being manifested that you are a letter of Christ" (2 Cor. 3:3).

Think of yourself as a letter and of Jesus as the envelope. When you, the letter, accepted Christ, you were put safe inside the envelope. "If any man is in Christ" (2 Cor. 5:17). The envelope was sealed with you inside it. "Having also believed, you were sealed in Him with the Holy Spirit of promise" (Eph. 1:13). We know where the envelope went. He went to a cross. He was nailed to it and died. Where was the letter? It was inside the envelope, and it also went to the cross. It was nailed to it and died. "I have been crucified with Christ" (Gal. 2:20). But that envelope also rose from the dead. What became true of the letter inside? It rose from the dead with the envelope. "It is no longer I who live, but Christ lives in me" (Gal. 2:20). Do you see? In regard to the new life, what is true of Christ is true of you. These are the facts of the new life. Next week's study will focus on these facts. This week we will discover the experience of the new life and what it looks like.

"In that day you shall know that I am in My Father, and you in Me, and I in you." John 14:20

DAY 2

Perhaps everyone has a soft spot for nostalgia. An old song, a photo album, the smell of autumn air, or a number of other things may produce in us a longing for things remembered. However, old things do not always have great sentimental value. Sometimes the old gets tossed in the trash, and the new becomes the preferred choice. Consider the following questions.

10. **Answer yes or no.**
    _____ A. Would you want to begin a new school year with an old notebook?
    _____ B. Would you try for an A+ performance this year with last year's term paper?
    _____ C. Would you hand out last year's school pictures if this year's were the best you'd ever had taken?
    _____ D. Would you wear smelly, dirty, work-in-the-yard clothes on a date with your favorite person?
    _____ E. Would you want to drink a glass of fresh milk if it had been mixed with an equal amount of sour milk?

In these instances the old and the new do not mix. The same is true with the new life you have been given in Christ. Today we will look at a parable of Jesus that illustrates the absurdity of trying to combine the old life with the new.

Read Luke 5:36-39.

11. **What would be your reaction to a friend who bought a brand new item of clothing, only to cut it up and use it to patch the holes in his or her old clothes?**

12. **Verse 36—According to Jesus, what would be the result in a situation like the one above (question 11)?**

13. **Has Jesus given you. . .**
    _____ A. fragments of His life to fill in the "holes" of your old sin nature
    or
    _____ B. a new life altogether

What do you think is the difference between A and B?

14. **What do you think is the danger of embracing only pieces of Christlikeness as your own?**

15. **Verse 37—What does Jesus say will happen to new wine when it is poured into old wine skins?**

16. **When you became a Christian, God "poured" Christ's life into you in the person of the Holy Spirit. What happens when you try to receive this new life while holding on to the old one? (Refer to question 15.)**

"Therefore if any man be in Christ, he is a new creature: old things are passed away; behold, all things are become new" (2 Cor. 5:17, KJV).

"All things are become new."

17. **Luke 5:37-38—Why must all things be made new?**

18. **Verse 39—What happens when we continue to partake of the old life?**

DAY 3

Read Colossians 3:5-17.

19. **What does the old life look like? Read verses 5, 8, and 9 again; then list specific deeds or characteristics that make up the old life.**

20. **Verse 6—What is God's response to such a life?**

21. **What actions do the following verses say you are to take in regard to the old life?**

    Verse 5

    Verse 8

    Verse 9

22. **What do you think this means?**

23. **What does the new life look like? Read verses 12-14; then list specific deeds or characteristics that make up the new life.**

24. **Verse 10—What do you think it means to put on the new self?**

When you think of putting on something, you might think of clothing. You put on a hat to cover your head. You put on gloves to cover your hands. In a way, we can relate this spiritual truth to putting on spiritual clothing. We might put on a "hat" of pure thoughts or "gloves" of humble service. You must remember, however, that when you put on the new life, you do not put it on with the option of taking it off. You put it on for good. And we do not pick and choose what we want to wear according to what mood we are in. We wear the whole outfit. We either clothe ourselves with all of Christ, or we do not clothe ourselves with any of Him.

25. **How do you think the following elements impact the new life?**

a. Lordship: how Christ's rule impacts the heart of the new life (v. 15)

b. Input: what goes into the new life (v. 16)

c. Motive: why the believer is to put on the new life (v. 17)

26. **Look back over question 19 and circle the things you listed which you continue to hold onto from the old life.**

27. **Look back over question 23 and circle the things you listed from the new life which you need to allow Christ to develop and mature in you.**

28. **What are some things you can do to remove the old (question 26) and embrace the new (question 27)? For your answer, refer to question 25.**

DAY 4

Read Ephesians 4:1-3,17-24.

The New American Standard translation compares the old life and the new life to a walk.

"I, therefore, the prisoner of the Lord, entreat you to walk in a manner worthy of the calling with which you have been called" (v. 1).
"This I say therefore, and affirm together with the Lord, that you walk no longer just as the Gentiles also walk, in the futility of their mind" (v. 17).

29. **What do you think is the significance of the word "walk" in regard to the old and new life?**

30. **Verses 17-19—How does Paul describe the walk of the old life?**

"But you did not learn Christ in this way" (Eph. 4:20).

31. **Verses 2-3,24—How does Paul describe the walk of the new life?**

32. **Verses 17-18—How do these verses describe the heart of one who does not walk with Christ?**

33. **Verse 19—And what follows?**

34. **How do you think obeying God's commands helps us to understand God Himself better?**

35. **Verse 23—How do you think this helps a person walk in the pattern of the new life?**

Think of someone you know who walks "in a manner worthy of the calling with which you have been called." Why has this person come to mind?

Now think of someone you know whose walk is futile, and whose heart is cold and hard toward Christ. Why has this person come to mind?

Take a few moments now to close your eyes and to pray for each of these two persons. What could you do for these persons in addition to prayer?

DAY 5

Read Titus 3:1-8.

36. **Verses 1-2—What does the new life look like in regard to our relationships with people?**

37. **Verse 3—"Enslaved to various lusts and pleasures." Though sin seems to promise freedom and fun, how does it actually make you its slave?**

38. **Verse 3—Look at the old life as it is described here. Does this look like fun? Does this look like something you would want to hold on to? Why do you think so many Christians embrace pieces of the old life?**

39. **Verses 4-5—What motivated God to save us?**

40. **Which of the following describes the greatest motivator for you to do right.**
    _____ I desire to do right to earn God's favor.
    _____ I desire to do right because I already have God's favor.
    Explain why you checked this one.

41. **Verse 7—What truth do you read in this verse?**

"He saved us from all that. It was all His doing; we had nothing to do with it. He gave us a bath, and we came out of it new people, washed inside and out by the Holy Spirit"[3] (Titus 3:5).

42. **Verse 5—He gave us a bath. How does this verse help us understand the new life?**

43. **Verse 5—"not on the basis of deeds." If deeds are not the basis for salvation, why do you think they are so significant after salvation? (Eph. 2:10 may help here.)**

44. **Titus 3:5-6—How has God equipped you to live the new life?**

"Not to us has it been given to have life in ourselves. For life we are wholly and continually dependent upon God, the Source and Fountain of life. Only by full dependence upon Him are the hidden potentialities of our natures realized. Apart from this we are but half-men, malformed and unbeautiful members of a noble race once made to wear the image of its Creator."[4] —A. W. Tozer

---

[1] Walter T. Conner, *The Gospel of Redemption* (Nashville: Broadman Press, 1945), 267.
[2] *Mere Christianity* by C. S. Lewis copyright © C. S. Lewis Pte. Ltd. 1942, 1943, 1944, 1952. Extract reprinted by permission.
[3] Eugene H. Peterson, *The Message* (Colorado Springs: NavPress, 1995).
[4] A. W. Tozer, *The Divine Conquest* (Urichsville, Ohio: Barbour and Company, 1950), 54-55.

WEEK 2
BECOMING WHO YOU ALREADY ARE

SCRIPTURE MEMORY
Who You Are in Christ
■ 2 Corinthians 5:21

DAY 1

Read Philippians 3:10-16.

1. How do each of the following verses describe the goal for which Paul was striving?

    verse 10

    verse 11

    verse 12

    verse 14

2. Look over what you just wrote. Describe in your own words what you understand to be the goal.

3. From memory, write the verse you memorized on "the believer's life."

4. Philippians 3:13—What elements of the new life do you also find in this verse?

5. According to the following verses, what does Paul understand to be true of himself?

    verse 12

    verse 13

6. In the following verses, what does Paul indicate about himself?

    verse 15a

    verse 16

7. Verse 14—"I press on toward the goal." What words or phrases from today's passage (Phil. 3:10-16) indicate that Paul had already reached the goal? And what words or phrases indicate the goal was

something for which he was striving? Write them under the correct heading below.

A goal already achieved   **A goal for which he was striving**

It is interesting. One minute Paul is writing as though this goal is something just beyond his grasp. The next minute he is writing as if he had grasped it already. Which one is true? Well, they both are true. Paul had attained perfection in Christ while at the same time he was becoming perfect. Not only was this true of Paul, it is also true of you. We will see scriptural truths of these principles in the rest of this week's study.

DAY 2

Read Romans 6:2-14.

8. **According to the following verses, what facts are true about Jesus Christ?**

   verse 9

   verse 10

9. **According to the following verses, how has God included you in Christ's history?**

   verse 4

   verse 5

   verse 6

   verse 8

10. **Based upon what you discovered in question 9, write what you understand to be true of yourself from God's perspective.**

"That we should no longer be slaves to sin" (v. 6).
"For sin shall not be master over you" (v. 14).

11. **Considering the passages above, what was our relationship to sin prior to coming to Christ?**

12. **Verse 7—What is true about a corpse? Why?**

"You cannot say to a slave, 'Live as a free man,' but you can say that to someone delivered from slavery. Now that we are in fact dead to sin—to its rule and reign—we are to count on that as being true. We are to keep before us this fact that we are no longer slaves. We can now stand up to sin and say no to it."[1]
—Jerry Bridges

13. Verse 11—Then what is true of our old self?

C. S. Lewis writes, "The more we get what we now call 'ourselves' out of the way and let Him take us over, the more truly ourselves we become. There is so much of Him that millions and millions of 'little Christs,' all different, will still be too few to express Him fully. He made them all. He invented—as an author invents characters in a novel—all the different men that you and I were intended to be. In that sense our real selves are all waiting for us in Him. It is no good trying to 'be myself' without Him. The more I resist Him and try to live on my own, the more I become dominated by my own heredity and upbringing and surroundings and natural desires. . .I am not, in my natural state, nearly so much of a person as I like to believe: most of what I call 'me' can be very easily explained. It is when I turn to Christ, when I give myself up to His Personality, that I first begin to have a real personality of my own. . .

Christ will indeed give you a real personality: but you must not go to Him for the sake of that. As long as your own personality is what you are bothering about you are not going to Him at all. The very first step is to try to forget about the self altogether. Your real, new self (which is Christ's and also yours, and yours just because it is His) will not come as long as you are looking for it. It will come when you are looking for Him. . .Give up yourself, and you find your real self. Lose your life and you will save it. . .Keep back nothing. Nothing that you have not given away will ever be really yours. Nothing in you that has not died will ever be raised from the dead. Look for yourself, and you will find in the long run only hatred, loneliness, despair, rage, ruin, and decay. But look for Christ and you will find Him, and with Him everything else thrown in."[2]

When you consider the physical birth or death of a person, you are dealing with facts. A person is born. A person dies. For example, the fact of an infant's birth is just as real to the mother on the days when she does not feel like being a mom as on the days when she does feel like it—when the baby cries as when the baby coos.

Christianity deals with the facts of life and death, too. Jesus' death was a fact as was His resurrection. The death and resurrection of Jesus Christ are historical events. It is a fact that He died. It is a fact that He arose from the dead. This passage teaches that you were included in His death. It is a fact that you died just as surely as Christ did. This passage also teaches that you were included in His resurrection. It is a fact that you rose from the dead just as Christ did. Whether or not you feel these facts to be true is of no significance. It does not change what is true.

14. Verse 6—So as a Christian, what is true about yourself? What are the facts, even as you give in to a particular sin?

It is crucial that you understand the facts of the new life. You will not know the experience of the new life until you understand the facts.

15. In verse 6, Paul writes, "knowing this." He goes on to emphasize the facts of the new life through verse 10. Then in verses 11 through 14 he writes how the Christian lives out these facts in the experience

of the new life. Write how we are to experience the new life according to verses 11-14.

Why must you understand that you already are dead before you will act as though you are dead to sin? Let us illustrate it this way. A person has a checking account. In the bank is deposited $500. This is the truth of his resources. These are the facts. Now based on these facts, he is able to spend or experience his resources. He writes a check for his car payment. He writes a check for a new CD. All the time he is keeping track of what he has spent in his checkbook register. But what if he decided to write in a different amount in the deposit column, let's say $200? He may not "experience" the resources of $500, but that would not change the fact that he had $500 in the bank. On the other hand, what if he did not know that the $500 was in his account? He would not experience the resources that he had because he would not know that they existed.

It is the same in the Christian life. Only your "account" does not represent riches for which you have worked. They are riches that have been accounted to you by grace. It is also an account that is always full, never to be depleted. All of Christ has been transferred to your account. How much holiness is in your account? Well, how holy is Jesus? How much perfection is in your account? How perfect is He? It does not change the facts on a day when you do not experience holiness. The facts are in the account. God is the "Banker." He has put the resources there in the Person of His Son. When He looks at you, He looks at the facts, what is in the account, not how you may be experiencing it. Unfortunately, most Christians are not aware of what is in the account. They never experience the new life because they do not know the facts. Tomorrow we will look at the account from God's perspective and discover just how rich we really are.

DAY 3

Yesterday we ended the study by comparing the new life to a bank account. Today we will focus on what has been accredited to us in this account.

"Blessed is he whose transgressions are forgiven, whose sins are covered. Blessed is the man whose sin the Lord does not count against him" (Ps. 32:1-2, NIV).

16. **When you came to Christ, what was the debt you brought with you as indicated in the above verses?**

17. **2 Corinthians 5:21—How does this contrast with who Jesus is?**

18. **2 Corinthians 5:21—Yet, what did Jesus become?**

19. 2 Corinthians 5:21—What is now true of you?

Interesting. We have this Person: Jesus; the only Person in the course of history who never sinned, ever. And in taking your sin, He gave you His righteousness. Never think of Christianity as only having your sins removed. This is only half of the story. Jesus took your sin on Himself, "He was numbered with the transgressors" (Isa. 53:12), and gave you His righteousness in its place, "that we might become the righteousness of God in Him" (2 Cor. 5:21).

What does God see when He looks at you? What does He see when He looks into your account? He sees a person whose sins have been forgiven; a person whose sins have been covered and overcome by the blood of His Son.

"Only let us live up to what we have already attained" *(Phil. 3:16, NIV).*

Are you beginning to see that this is God's perspective of you? These are the facts. Now it is a matter of living up to who you already are—a child of God— His own because of what Christ Jesus has done for you.

Let us look at some other passages that will help us understand how God sees us.

20. Next to the corresponding Scripture reference, write the facts each passage reveals about you before Jesus took your place and the facts that are true about you now.

	Facts Before Jesus Took Your Place	Facts About You Now
Romans 9:25-26		
1 Corinthians 3:17	N/A	
Galatians 4:7		
1 John 4:17	N/A	

21. How does your new identity motivate you to live? Explain.

DAY 4

Read 1 Peter 2:9-10.

22. According to today's passage, who are you?

Notice how today's passage echoes the covenant that God made with the nation of Israel in the Old Testament.

"'"Now then, if you will indeed obey My voice and keep My covenant, then you shall be My own possession among all the peoples, for all the earth is Mine; and you shall be to Me a kingdom of priests and a holy nation. These are the words that you shall speak to the sons of Israel"'" (Ex. 19:5-6).

23. **When you make something—whether it is a cake, a table, a dress, a project at school—what is the significance of having a picture of what the finished result will look like?**

24. **In the process of making it, what causes you to look at the picture of the finished work?**

25. **What does the finished work of a Christian look like? (Refer to questions 19, 20b, and 22.)**

26. **How might understanding the perspective that God has of all believers (question 25) help you when you are tempted to be judgmental toward another believer?**

27. **Verse 9—"that you may proclaim the excellencies of Him." Look again at v. 9. Why does Peter tell his readers who they are before he tells them what they are to do? (Refer to questions 23-24.)**

28. **Some people might think, "Why would I want to tell another believer that he or she is already perfect in Christ? Wouldn't that just cause him or her to be lazy and not do anything for Him? Wouldn't he or she see that as a license to sin?" How would you respond? (Refer to question 21.)**

> "God has not given us the power to imitate Him. He has made us partakers of His nature so that we can actually be like Him. You don't become a Christian by acting like one. We are not on a performance basis with God. He doesn't say, 'Here are my standards, now you measure up.' He knows you can't solve the problem of an old sinful nature simply by improving your behavior. He must change your nature, give you an entirely new self—the life of Christ in you—which is the grace you need to measure up to His standards."[5]
> —Neil T. Anderson

DAY 5

This week we have focused mostly on who we are in Christ: the facts of the Christian life. And we have discovered that, beginning to end, it is accomplished in Christ. God regards the facts of Jesus' life as the facts of your life. There is nothing left for you to do to impress God. He already sees you as perfect, and you cannot add to perfection.

The Christian *experience*, then is simply a matter of living out each day what is already true of you. And once again, God has not left you alone to figure that out. He has given you His Spirit to indwell you—His very life to empower you to be who you are. Today we will discover the tools He has given us to equip us to be more like Him in our daily experience.

Read 2 Peter 1:3-4.

29. Verse 3—"Seeing that His divine power has granted to us everything pertaining to life and godliness." Why must you understand that any hope for godly living in this world is to be found in Him and not in you?

30. According to verse 3, what does godliness come through? (check one)

_____ improving yourself
_____ knowing God

Explain.

"Everything that goes into a life of pleasing God has been miraculously given to us by getting to know, personally and intimately, the One who invited us to God. The best invitation we ever received! We were also given absolutely terrific promises to pass on to you, your tickets to participation in the life of God after you turned your back on a world corrupted by lust" (2 Pet. 1:3-4).

31. How do you think a person comes to know God personally and intimately?

32. Match the following verses with the corresponding tools which equip us to become more mature Christians in our daily experience.

_____ 1 Corinthians 14:20   a. Trials/testing of your faith
_____ Colossians 1:28   b. The Word of God
_____ 2 Timothy 3:16-17   c. Obedience to the Word
_____ James 1:2-4   d. Help of mature Christians
_____ 1 John 2:5   e. Mature thinking

33. Which of the above is the most difficult for you to submit yourself? Explain.

34. "He has granted to us his precious and magnificent promises, in order that by them you might become partakers of the divine nature" (2 Pet. 1:4). Of the promises you have discovered this week, which ones are the most encouraging to you to become more like Christ in your daily experience? Explain.

Explanation of the Puzzle Illustration
The Facts and the Experience of the Christian Life
The facts and the experience of the Christian life can be illustrated by the completed picture and the individual pieces of a jigsaw puzzle. It is easy to see

our Christian experience in the scattered puzzle pieces on the table. The labor of producing proper speech, a pure thought life, Christlike actions in our lives is as tedious as interlocking specific puzzle pieces together. We think we must work on one aspect of our character before we can move on to the next. Putting a puzzle together is hard work. Imagine the added difficulty of putting it together without any idea of what the finished product would look like, without the picture on a box top to use as a reference. This would be next to impossible.

When it comes to living a Christlike life, we sometimes feel as if we have no reference point—no complete picture of godliness by which to model our lives. So we begin the futile attempt of putting the pieces together blindly, and we get discouraged. We have learned that we do have a reference. The reference is Jesus. In Christ we have a completed picture of the puzzle box top.

Now, here is the question. Which is true of you? Is your Christian life the completed picture or the pieces on the table? Well, both are true. You are the completed picture—the facts of the Christian life. At the same time, you are the pieces—the experience of the Christian life. You will not experience the character of the Christian life until you understand the facts. Facts do not depend on experience, but experience depends on the facts. This is why Paul wrote in Philippians 3:14, "Only let us live up to what we have already attained."

Only let us live up (the experience of the new life)

to what we have already attained (the facts of the new life)

It is important that you see your life in the context of these principles. It is important that you also see the studies in this book in the context of these principles. When you study wholeheartedness, sexual morality, and other topics, remember that in Christ God already sees you as perfect. You must accept these facts as true of yourself and live up to that perfection in your daily experience.

(The characteristics included in the puzzle illustration are not intended to be an exhaustive list. Rather, they reflect areas of Christlikeness which we will focus on in this book.)

[1] Reprinted from *The Pursuit of Holiness*. © 1978 by Jerry Bridges. Used by permission of NavPress, Colorado Springs, CO. All rights reserved.

[2] *Mere Christianity* by C. S. Lewis copyright © C. S. Lewis Pte. Ltd. 1942, 1943, 1944, 1952. Extract reprinted by permission.

[3] Watchman Nee, *The Normal Christian Life* (Wheaton, Illinois: Tyndale House Publishers, 1977), 75.

[4] Taken from *His Imprint, My Expression*. Copyright © 1996 by Kay Arthur. Published by Harvest House Publishers, Eugene, Oregon 97402. Used by permission.

[5] Neil T. Anderson, *Victory Over the Darkness* (Ventura, California: Regal Books, 1990), 74.

[6] Eugene H. Peterson, *The Message* (Colorado Springs: Navpress, 1993, 1994, 1995).

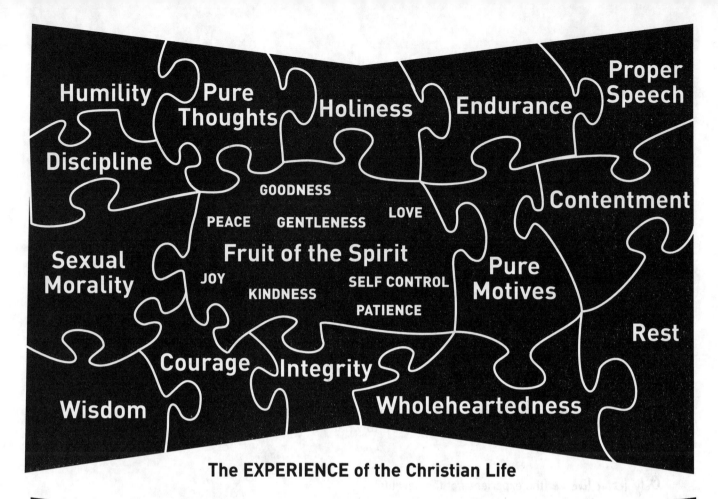

The EXPERIENCE of the Christian Life

Humility Pure Thoughts Holiness Endurance Proper Speech

Discipline

GOODNESS

PEACE GENTLENESS LOVE

Contentment

Sexual Morality

Fruit of the Spirit

JOY SELF CONTROL

KINDNESS

PATIENCE

Pure Motives

Rest

Courage Integrity

Wisdom Wholeheartedness

The FACTS of the Christian Life

WEEK 3
A NEW ATTITUDE

DAY 1

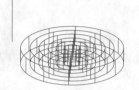

1. **Next to the following verses, write the specific sin(s) mentioned and God's attitude toward them.**

	Sin(s) Mentioned	God's Attitude
Psalm 11:5		
Proverbs 6:16-19		
Proverbs 11:1		
Zechariah 8:17		

2. **How does God's attitude, as revealed in the above passages, compare with what you observe as the world's attitude toward sin?**

3. **According to the following verses, what characterizes the fool's attitude toward sin?**

   Proverbs 10:23

   Proverbs 14:9

4. **Psalm 53:1—What characterizes the fool according to this verse?**

5. **Under the correct headings below, write the attitude revealed toward God and toward sin.**

	Attitude Toward God	Attitude Toward Sin
Psalm 97:10		
Proverbs 8:13		
Proverbs 16:6		

6. How would you briefly summarize what should be a Christian's attitude toward God and his or her attitude toward sin? Why do you think this is true? (John 3:19-21 may help here. Also refer to questions 3, 4, and 5.)

DAY 2

Yesterday we contrasted God's attitude toward sin with the world's attitude toward sin. If we are to pursue Christlikeness, we must reject the world's light-hearted view and embrace the hatred of sin that God has in regard to sins in our lives. Today we will deepen our understanding of what it means to hate sin.

Read Amos 5:14-15.

7. "Seek good and not evil" (v. 14). Why do you think you must seek good—take some initiative in finding it and doing it—rather than waiting on the good to find you?

"If you do well, will not your countenance be lifted up? And if you do not do well, sin is crouching at the door; and its desire is for you, but you must master it" (Gen. 4:7).

8. What picture does the above verse give of sin? (Compare with question 7.)

9. Amos 5:14—According to this verse, what are the results that come from seeking good?

Amos 5:15 begins with the command to hate evil. Romans 12:9 records a similar command: "Abhor what is evil; cling to what is good."

The word abhor here means to consider evil or sin repulsive. Notice what Walter A. Henrichsen writes about this.

"Close your eyes for a moment and think of something that really nauseates you. That feeling is the word that Paul is using when he says "abhor." God wants you to view sin like you view the thing you're thinking about right now. That's what God wants your attitude to be. You can hardly contain yourself. You almost begin to gag you hate it so badly. . .Everyone is plagued with some sin, but some Christians don't hate evil. As a matter of fact they have little pet sins they embrace to their bosoms. They play with them and pet them."[2]

10. From what you know of sin, why are the ones in your life worthy of such hatred?

11. Do you have sins in your life which really bother you and others which you treat rather flippantly? Explain.

Is it your aim not to sin or not to sin very much?

"One day. . .I realized that deep within my heart my real aim was not to sin very much. I found it difficult to say, 'Yes, Lord, from here on I will make it my aim not to sin.' . . .Can you imagine a soldier going into battle with the aim of 'not getting hit very much'? The very suggestion is ridiculous. His aim is not to get hit at all! Yet if we have not made a commitment to holiness without exception, we are like a soldier going into battle with the aim of not getting hit very much."[4] —Jerry Bridges

12. Think about the sins with which you sometimes struggle.

impure thoughts	anger	hate	selfishness
immorality	pride	stealing	cheating
impure talk	greed	worry/anxiety	jealousy
impure motives	laziness	lying	dishonoring your parents
critical spirit	rebellion	being judgmental	others

13. Using what you have learned today, write a prayer about the sins you are struggling with.

"Abhor what is evil; cling to what is good" (Rom. 12:9).
"Hate evil, love good" (Amos 5:15).

14. In your own life, how does loving what is good affect hating what is evil?

DAY 3

15. What are recent things in your life that have brought anxiety or unrest?

16. How did the worry over these things affect you physically?

17. Read Psalm 38:18. Over what was David troubled?

18. How does this compare with what you wrote on question 15?

"When we sin as the image-bearers of God, we are saying to the whole of creation, to all of nature under our dominion, to the birds of the air and the beasts of the field: 'This is how God is. This is how your creator behaves. Look in this mirror; look at us and you will see the character of the Almighty.' We say to the world, 'God is covetous; God is ruthless; God is bitter; God is a murderer, a thief, a slanderer, an adulterer. God is all of these things that we are doing.'"[3]
—R. C. Sproul

Read Psalm 32:3-5.

19. How does David describe his own physical trauma in the following verses? (Compare with question 16.)

    verse 3

    verse 4

20. Verse 3—What brought about these illnesses?

21. Verse 5—What happened here?

22. What are the effects of sin in your life?

23. Verse 5—What brings these effects to a halt? Why?

"Many are the sorrows of the wicked. But he who trusts in the Lord, lovingkindness shall surround him" (Ps. 32:10).

DAY 4

Read Psalm 36:1-4.

24. Verse 1—What is the ungodly person's attitude toward God?

25. Verse 4—What is his attitude toward evil?

26. Verse 1—As indicated in this verse, to what voice does the ungodly person listen? (check one)
    _____ The voice of God
    _____ The voice of transgression or sin

Notice the following paraphrases of Psalm 36:2.

"He has smooth-talked himself into believing that his evil will never be noticed."[5]

"He thinks too much of himself. He doesn't see his sin and hate it."[6]

"Instead, in their conceit, they think they can hide their evil deeds and not get caught."[7]

27. Considering the above paraphrases, what does the voice of transgression or sin communicate to the ungodly?

28. Yet, what is really true? (Refer to Eccl. 11:9.)

29. Psalm 36:3—How has listening to the voice of transgression or sin corrupted his mouth?

30. Verse 3b—How has listening to this voice (question 26) affected his ability to determine what is true?

In the beginning, transgression doesn't speak with a blatant voice such as, "Commit murder. Embezzle money. Commit adultery." Rather, transgression gets its foothold in much more subtle ways. It brings in an element that sounds like the truth to justify the act. Such as . . .
- "I'm not really lying; I'm just stretching the truth."
- "It's OK to take a few dollars. She has so much money, she'll never even know it's missing."
- "So what if I cheat on my time sheet. They don't pay me enough anyway."
- "Yes, I made her mad, but she deserved it and I'm having a bad day."
- "Yeah, I made a lot of hollow promises in the campaign, but that's just politics."
- "If she doesn't lose her virginity to me, she'll just end up losing it to someone who doesn't really care about her."

31. Think of other examples like the ones above that make sin easy to justify.

"He commits himself to an evil course. . ." (Ps. 36:4).

32. How do you think "little" sins in a person's life might lead a person onto a path of more and more sin?

33. To where does this path lead? (Refer to Jas. 1:14-15.)

34. Why is sin worthy of your hatred?

"Let no man think lightly of sin. Though it can be forgiven and swept away, and the gross sinner may become the great saint, there will be scars and bitter memories and habits surging up again after we thought they were dead; and the old ache and fever that we caught in the pestilential land will hang by us when we have migrated into a more wholesome climate."[10] —Alexander Maclaren

"When an ancient temptation or trial becomes an approved feature in the culture, a way of life that is expected and encouraged, Christians have a stumbling block put before them that is hard to recognize for what it is, for it has been made into a monument, gilded with bronze and bathed in decorative lights. It has become an object of veneration. But the plain fact is that it is right in the middle of the road of faith, obstructing discipleship. For all its fancy dress and honored position it is still a stumbling block."[8]
—Eugene Peterson

35. From memory, write the verse you memorized on "who you are in Christ."

36. As we discovered last week, Jesus became sin so that you could become righteous. And what is God's attitude toward sin?

You can think of it this way: Jesus was hated so that you could be loved!

"My God My God, why hast Thou forsaken me?" (Matt. 27:46).

"For you know the grace of our Lord Jesus Christ, that though He was rich, yet for your sake He became poor, that you through His poverty might become rich" (2 Cor. 9:8).

The cross tells us that God does not deal lightly with sin. He hates it.

We must not deal lightly with sin either.

37. Psalm 141:4—What impact do you think your friends have on your attitude toward sin?

38. Psalm 119:136—What was the psalmist's attitude toward the sin of disobedience?

39. How does this differ from your attitude toward sin?

40. Would you like to feel more like the psalmist did as he wrote Psalm 119:136? How can you reach that point?

Read Psalm 51:3-4.

41. Verse 3—In this verse, what does David say in regard to his sin?

42. How do you relate to him after completing this study?

43. Verse 4—According to the first part of this verse, what did David understand about sin?

Do you see? It is time to leave the comparisons behind. You may look OK when comparing yourself with everyone else. You may be able to generate enough "good" on the surface to be accepted by your peers. As a matter of fact, no one else may even have a clue about the sins you struggle with in your life. But God knows. And they are evil in His sight! What sin is worth holding onto? Let them all go.

"If we confess our sins, He is faithful and righteous to forgive us our sins and to cleanse us from all unrighteousness" (1 John 1:9).

44. Allow the Holy Spirit time now to expose your sins to you. As He reveals them to you, confess them out loud. As you obey in confessing your sins, write what you experience in the space below.

"Come now, and let us reason together, says the Lord, though your sins are as scarlet, they will be as white as snow; though they are red like crimson, they will be like wool" (Isa. 1:18).

[1] Walter T. Conner, *The Gospel of Redemption* (Nashville: Broadman Press, 1945), 20.

[2] Walter A. Henrichsen, *Many Aspire Few Attain* (Colorado Springs: Navpress), 12-13.

[3] R. C. Sproul, *The Holiness of God* (Wheaton, Illinois: Tyndale House Publishers, 1985), 152.

[4] Reprinted from *The Pursuit of Holiness.* © 1978 by Jerry Bridges. Used by permission of NavPress, Colorado Springs, CO. All rights reserved.

[5] Eugene H. Peterson, *The Message* (Colorado Springs: Navpress, 1993, 1994, 1995).

[6] *The Everyday Bible, New Century Version* (Dallas: Word Publishing, 1987, 1988).

[7] *The Living Bible* (Wheaton, Illinois: Tyndale House Publishers, 1971, 1973).

[8] Eugene Peterson, *A Long Obedience in the Same Direction* (Downers Grove, Illinois: InterVarsity Press, 1980), 146-147. Used by permission.

[9] *The Student Bible, New International Version* (Grand Rapids, Michigan: Zondervan Bible Publishers, 1986).

[10] Alexander Maclaren, *Expositions of Holy Scripture: Luke* (Grand Rapids, Michigan: Baker Book House, 1974, 1977), 196.

God provides a way out

WEEK 4
TEMPTATION

SCRIPTURE MEMORY
Temptation
■ Matthew 26:41
■ 1 Corinthians 10:13
■ James 4:7

DAY 1

This week we will discover what the Bible teaches on the subject of temptation. We will observe how Jesus responded to temptation. We will see its limitations and how we may overcome it. Today's passage reveals one of the sources of temptation and how temptation breeds sin.

Read James 1:13-15.

1. Verse 13—What does this verse say about God?

2. Verse 13—What is wrong with the statement, "God is making it hard for me to be good"?

3. Verse 14—According to this verse, what is one of the sources of temptation?

4. Verse 15—When "lust" and "the will" get married, what kind of children do they produce?

5. Verse 15—In its infancy stage, sin is a mere choice. Then it matures into a single transgression. When it is full-grown it becomes a habit. And ultimately, as sin is "accomplished," what happens?

6. What could happen if "the will" were to choose another mate in the beginning rather than tying the knot with "lust"?
(Refer to question 4.)

7. What do you think would be the ideal marriage for the will?

DAY 2

Today we will witness one of the most significant accounts of Jesus' manhood in Scripture. Right after His baptism and just before His public ministry begins, the Adversary rears his ugly head.

Read Matthew 4:1-11.

8. Verse 1—Who was the source of the temptations Jesus faced?

9. Next to each verse and under the correct column, write the temptation recorded and Jesus' response.

Temptation	Jesus' Response
Verse 3	Verse 4
Verse 6	Verse 7
Verses 8-9	Verse 10

10. What impresses you about Jesus' response to temptation here?

11. Why would the words "suggestion to sin" be an accurate description of what temptation is?

12. At this point Jesus, the human being, had known the security of a quiet home in Nazareth where He could study, learn Scripture, and enjoy regular worship. His life was that of a normal Jew with a low profile. Then He is baptized, and a voice from heaven confirms that He is God's Son. This is a significant moment! Immediately Satan is on the scene! (Notice Matthew 3:17 and Matthew 4:1.) What do you think this says about the enemy and the timing of his attacks on believers today?

13. Verses 2-3—How does Satan try to take advantage of a seemingly "weak" moment in Jesus' life?

14. What does this indicate about Satan, what he knows about you and how he attacks you?

15. Verse 3—" 'If you are the Son of God.' " Here he tries to tempt Jesus into doubting that He is God. When has Satan tempted you to doubt about God?

16. Verse 5—Satan takes Jesus to Jerusalem to the pinnacle of the Temple—a place that may seem off limits to Satan. Why must we be extra cautious in regard to his attack in churches today?

17. Verses 8-9—In the first two temptations Satan was subtle; yet how does he tempt Jesus here?

"New believers often think that temptation itself is sin. They are mistaken. There is no sin in being tempted; there is sin only in yielding to temptation. This is a comfort even for the severely tempted. This is added encouragement if you remember that the Lord Jesus, though tempted gloriously triumphed and overcame. The Head has triumphed and the members share in the victory."[1]
—Walter T. Conner

> "Purity demands that we know ahead of time what we will do when temptation comes. The ordinary Christian will probably not make a spiritual decision under the duress of temptation. . .Our safest course is to avoid temptation entirely. . .Strength comes before, not during, temptation. Overcoming is a prior act. Know ahead of time which lusts are your greatest weaknesses."[2]
> —Christopher B. Adsit

18. Look again at Jesus' responses to the temptations. (Refer to question 9.) Jesus never gets into a debate with Satan. He never argues with him about sin. He simply faces each temptation by quoting a verse in the face of the enemy. What does this say to you about responding to temptation today?

Notice how the devil responds. He doesn't hang around and tempt Jesus over and over with the same sins. He moves on. Yes, he is persistent with his tempting. But once the Scripture is quoted, he moves on to a different temptation and he eventually moves out (v. 11).

19. From memory, write the verse you memorized on "hating sin."

20. How could you use this verse the next time you are tempted to sin?

"For we do not have a high priest who cannot sympathize with our weaknesses, but one who has been tempted in all things as we are, yet without sin" (Heb. 4:15).

DAY 3

Read Matthew 26:41.

21. What wisdom do you see in one praying that he or she would not be led into temptation as opposed to one praying that he or she would not be led into sin?

22. "Keep watching and praying." Can you ever let down your guard in regard to temptation? Why or why not? (Refer to 1 Cor. 10:12.)

> "We sometimes think that the higher one goes in the moral and spiritual life, the less subject to temptation he will be. This is not true, as every Christian knows who has made any progress in spiritual matters and as the example of the Savior himself shows. It would be nearer the truth to say that the higher one goes in the spiritual life the subtler and stronger does temptation become."[3] —C. S. Lewis

23. How do circumstances and environment lend themselves to temptation?

24. Think of a sin which the Holy Spirit has convicted you of recently. What circumstances or surroundings assist in tempting you to give in to this again?

"Do not enter the path of the wicked, and do not proceed in the way of evil men. Avoid it, do not pass by it; turn away from it and pass on" (Prov. 4:14-15).

"But put on the Lord Jesus Christ, and make no provision for the flesh in regard to its lusts" (Rom. 13:14).

25. According to Romans 13:14, what two actions are you to take in regard to temptation?

26. What do you think it means to "put on the Lord Jesus Christ"?

27. What do you think it means to "make no provision for the flesh in regard to its lusts"? (Eph. 4:27 may help here.)

28. Read Matthew 26:41. Why can't you overcome temptation on your own, in your own strength?

29. What must you do instead? (refer to question 26)

DAY 4

Read James 4:6-8.

Today's passage emphasizes the actions we are to take in regard to temptation.

30. According to the following verses, what actions are we to take that will put ourselves at God's disposal?

Verse 7

Verse 8

31. Verse 8— How does God respond to these actions?

32. Verse 7–According to this verse, what action are we to take against Satan?

33. Verse 7—And how does Satan respond to this action?

If you know that you have a hard time with alcohol, don't spend your time with friends who drink. If sexual sin is a problem for you, don't spend time alone with your date. If overeating is something you can't seem to get victory over, don't go out and buy a bunch of candy bars, put them in your room, and then pray for God to keep you from eating them.[4]

"No man knows how bad he is till he has tried very hard to be good. A silly idea is current that good people do not know what temptation means. This is an obvious lie. Only those who try to resist temptation know how strong it is. After all, you find out the strength of the German army by fighting against it, not by giving in. You find out the strength of a wind by trying to walk against it, not by lying down. A man who gives in to temptation after five minutes simply does not know what it would have been like an hour later. That is why bad people, in one sense, know very little about badness. They have lived a sheltered life by always giving in. We never find out the strength of the evil impulse inside us until we try to fight it: and Christ, because He was the only man who never yielded to temptation, is also the only man who knows to the full what temptation means—the only complete realist."[5]
—C. S. Lewis

34. How do you think a believer draws near to God?

35. How do you think a believer can resist Satan?

36. "I don't know how it feels to resist Satan. To tell you the truth I don't really even know what it feels like to be tempted." What do you think this statement reveals about this person?

37. Look again at today's passage. Do you think it is possible to draw near to God without resisting Satan? Is it possible to resist Satan without drawing nearer to God? Explain.

38. "Cleanse your hands." How will drawing near to God and resisting Satan affect our response toward outward sins?

39. "Purify your hearts." How will drawing near to God and resisting Satan affect our response toward inward sins?

40. If you are resisting God, to whom does verse 7 indicate you are submitting yourself?

Remember that the flesh is weak (Matt. 26:41). It doesn't have the strength or the capacity to be in control. It must submit itself to something: the Spirit or the Adversary.

DAY 5

Read 1 Corinthians 10:13.

41. What does this verse say about temptation?

42. What does it say about God?

43. "No temptation has overtaken you but such as is common to man." How does the truth of this encourage you?

Yet, how might Satan use this truth to justify your sin?

44. "But with the temptation will provide the way of escape also." Satan may hold you in his trap, but God always provides a trap door. Whose choice is it to use the trap door? Explain.

God doesn't force His way. But He does provide the way.

45. Why do you think people might choose not to use the trap door or the escape that God has given them?

Tony Evans writes, "The only reason you and I don't escape sometimes is that we are too much in love with the temptation. We want the temptation, so we don't want the escape.

So what do we do? We play with the temptation rather than hitting the exit. God builds immediate exit doors to get you out of a temptation if you want to get out. But if you don't want to escape, if you would rather crave evil things, God will discipline you."[6]

Read Psalm 124:7-8.

46. Verse 7—How are you like the bird here in regard to temptation?

47. Only an outside source can come along and loosen the snare. The bird cannot release itself. What is the outside source that loosens the snare of temptation? (v. 8)

"The Lord knows how to rescue the godly from temptation"
(2 Pet. 2:9).

48. Whose choice is it to fly away?

[1] Walter T. Conner, *The Gospel of Redemption* (Nashville: Broadman Press, 1945), 6.
[2] Christopher B. Adsit, *Personal Disciple-Making* (Nashville: Thomas Nelson Publishers, 1993), 296.
[3] *Mere Christianity* by C. S. Lewis copyright © C. S. Lewis Pte. Ltd. 1942, 1943, 1944, 1952. Extract reprinted by permission.
[4] Tony Evans, *Returning to Your First Love* (Chicago: Moody Press, 1995), 151-152. Used by permission.
[5] Lewis, *Mere Christianity*.
[6] Evans, *Returning to Your First Love*.

Jesus did only what was holy

WEEK 5
HOLINESS

SCRIPTURE MEMORY
Holiness
- ■ 2 Corinthians 7:1
- ■ 1 Thessalonians 4:7
- ■ 1 Peter 1:14-15

DAY 1

Holiness in man is stressed throughout the Scriptures. God requires that His children be separated or set apart, dedicated exclusively to Himself. This holiness is especially manifested in the character and conduct of the believer as he or she continues to grow toward Christlikeness. It is God's gracious work that makes this possible, and your own free will allows you to experience it.

Read 1 Peter 1:14-19.

1. From memory, write the verse you memorized on "the believer's life."

2. 1 Peter 1:14-15—We have studied that the believer's life is not merely turning away from what is evil, but is also turning toward what is good. How do these verses uphold these principles of the new life?

3. What do you think is indicated in verse 15 about. . .

inward holiness: "be holy yourselves"

outward holiness: "in all your behavior"

So far Peter has stated the "what" in regard to holiness. In the rest of today's passage he answers the "why."

4. How does each phrase from today's passage motivate you to be holy and to live a holy life?

a. Verse 16: "for I am holy"

b. Verse 17: "the One who impartially judges according to each man's work"

c. Verses 18-19: "you were not redeemed with perishable things. . .but with. . .the blood of Christ"

5. "Conduct yourselves in fear during the time of your stay upon earth."
How can a healthy fear produce a holy conduct?

"Therefore, having these promises, beloved, let us cleanse ourselves from all defilement of flesh and spirit, perfecting holiness in the fear of God" (2 Cor. 7:1).

DAY 2

Read 1 Thessalonians 4:7.

6. **For what purpose have we been called?**

"The destined end of man is not happiness, nor health, but holiness."[1]
—Oswald Chambers

7. **If a person considers happiness to be the goal of life, how might holiness be compromised in his or her life?**

8. **How do you think holiness relates to a person's "whole-ness"?**

Read 1 Corinthians 3:16-17.

In the Old Testament, the dwelling place of God was the temple in Jerusalem. It had been constructed with divine instructions. But this temple was a material structure. In Christ, the spiritual temple supersedes the material. As a believer, you are His temple. You are the dwelling place of the God who created the earth!

This is a difficult concept to grasp: God dwelling in you as opposed to God dwelling in a building. Maybe the following illustration will shed some light in helping us understand it.

9. **Which do you think represents the true dwelling place of the sun?**
   a. a house: where, for instance, it shines in through the windows
   or
   b. a flower blossom: produced from the sun's indwelling
   Explain.

   Can a building really contain the glory of the sun?

"And this is the message we have heard from Him and announce to you, that God is light, and in Him there is no darkness at all" (1 John 1:5).

10. Understanding this characteristic of God, what type of dwelling place or temple is worthy of His presence?

11. Read 1 Corinthians 3:17. How does Paul describe the temple of God?

12. So who has ownership and maintenance rights over this temple?

    Why? (Refer also to 1 Cor. 6:19-20.)

13. What do you think are examples of specific sins that are committed against the true temple of God, the body of the believer?

14. Read 1 Corinthians 3:17. What are consequences of these and other sins committed against the temple of God?

15. How does today's study encourage your pursuit of holiness?

DAY 3

Holiness is a concept that is difficult to grasp. Often it is taught in relationship to what it is not. Aside from His moral perfection, God's holiness encompasses everything that makes Him God and not man: His "otherness."

"There is no one holy like the Lord, indeed, there is no one besides Thee, nor is there any rock like our God" (1 Sam. 2:2).

If holiness is intangible when studying the character of God, how can we begin to grasp it in relationship to ourselves? How can we know what holiness looks like in a human being? The answers lie in the gospels. Jesus was the perfect embodiment of holiness. Any page in the Bible that gives us a glimpse of His life and the way He lived it will give us a lesson on holiness.

Jesus never settled for what was good. He did only what was holy. What is the difference between the two? Where is the dividing line? Today's passage will show us the heart of Christ and the single motive for everything Jesus did while here on earth.

Read John 8:26-29.

16. Imagine that you have access to all the knowledge in the world for one hour. There is no limit to this access. What are some dilemmas or crises in the world for which you would find the answers? (You might think of things that deal with medical research, the future, international relations, or others.)

17. In your estimation, what good would come to the world as a result of the knowledge you had been given?

18. Jesus Christ is God in the flesh (John 1:14). He is omniscient. This means He is all-knowing. He has access to all knowledge past, present, and future. When He was here on earth, He had all of the answers to the questions that faced His generation and He had (and has) all of the answers to the questions that face our generation: the things you just wrote about. Of all the things He could have shared with the world, what was the determining factor for what He did share? (John 8:26-27)

Where is your commitment? To morality? The unsaved? The poor? The ministry? The church? Education? Political issues? A vocation? A person? To God's will? To God Himself?

19. Verse 26—To what will a holy ear tune itself? What will a holy mouth utter?

20. What do you think happens when the ear and mouth settle for what is good rather than for what is holy?

21. Verse 28—Where did Jesus' actions originate?

22. Verse 28—If we are to know the difference between what is good and what is holy, from whom must we be learning?

23. Verse 28—" 'When you lift up the Son of Man, then you will know that I am He.' " Jesus is making reference to His crucifixion. What do you think His example teaches us about holiness in suffering?

24. At this point you may be thinking, "There is no way. I cannot be holy the way Jesus was holy." But who is your Companion as you pursue holiness, and what does Jesus say about Him? (v. 29)

25. " 'For I always do the things that are pleasing to Him.' " What impresses you about Jesus and His statement here?

" 'I do nothing on My own initiative,
But I speak these things as the Father taught Me. . .
For I always do the things that are pleasing to Him'" (John 8:28-29).

"The Lord Jesus Christ refused to be committed to the parochial need of His own day and generation. . .He was not committed to the pressing social problems of His time... Christ was not even committed to the needs of a perishing world; He was neither unmindful nor unmoved by all these other issues, but as Perfect Man He was committed to His Father, and for that only to which His Father was committed in Him—exclusively!"[3]
—W. Ian Thomas

26. Look at the above statements of holiness from today's passage. What difference would there be if you lived by them for a single day of your life?

27. What is stopping you from committing today to these purposes?

DAY 4

Read Hebrews 12:2,14-17.

28. What is likely to become of a pre-med student who is half-hearted about pursuing his or her degree?

What is likely to become of the athlete who is lazy in pursuing his or her training?

29. Verse 14—"Pursue. . .sanctification." How do we know when holiness or sanctification is truly the goal? (Refer to question 28.)

"Holiness is not an experience; it is the re-integration of our character, the rebuilding of a ruin. It is skilled labor, a long-term project, demanding everything God has given us for life and godliness."[5] —Sinclair B. Ferguson

30. What would a blind person miss in an art gallery?

31. Why does a spiritually blind person overlook God?

32. Verse 2—When we fix our eyes on Jesus, whom do we see?

33. Verse 14—When does the heart become an organ that sees?

"Blessed are the poor in heart, for they shall see God'" (Matt. 5:8).

"Only the holy will see God. Holiness is a prerequisite to heaven. Perfection is a requirement for eternity. We wish it weren't so. We act like it isn't so. We act like those who are 'decent' will see God. We suggest that those who try hard will see God. We act as if we're good if we never do anything too bad. And that goodness is enough to qualify us for heaven.
Sounds right to us, but it doesn't sound right to God. And He sets the standard."[6] —Max Lucado

"But the one who hates his brother is in the darkness and walks in the darkness, and does not know where he is going because the darkness has blinded his eyes" (1 John 2:9).

People are eternal beings. Christ died for people. And every person has the potential of being a place where God can make His home. The one who is spiritually farsighted has lost the perspective of people and how valuable they are to God.

34. According to the following verses, what are things that can prevent spiritual farsightedness?

Hebrews 12:14a

Hebrews 12:15

People who are spiritually nearsighted can't see things beyond a short range. They have a perspective only of what is up close: temporal things. Esau suffered from spiritual nearsightedness. By his birthright as the first-born, he not only would receive the honors of inheritance in relationship to rank within his earthly family, but would also carry on the promises made to Abraham in the spiritual sense. But Esau sacrificed the eternal for the temporal. "He sold his own birthright for a single meal" (v. 16).

35. With this in mind, how do you think Christians are tempted with spiritual nearsightedness today—exchanging the glory of heaven for worldly pleasures?

36. Do we have any hope of 20/20 spiritual vision? Can we be fitted with a heart of holiness that will allow us to see God? What is the answer according to Hebrews 12:1-2?

"The whole purpose of God in redemption is to make us holy and to restore us to the image of God."[7] —A. W. Tozer

DAY 5

Read 2 Kings 4:8-17.

37. Verse 8—Who does Elisha the prophet encounter in Shunem and what happens in this verse?

38. Verse 9—What does the woman conclude about Elisha?

39. What do you think the woman saw in Elisha's life that would cause her to draw this conclusion?

40. Since she was able to see these things in Elisha, what might this reveal about her own life?

41. How does she extend the boundaries of hospitality? (2 Kings 4:9-11)

42. Verse 9, "And she said to her husband. . ." What do you think the Shunammite husband saw in his wife that would cause him to trust her judgment and her motives?

43. 2 Kings 4:12-13—How did Elisha respond to the woman's kindness?

44. Verses 14-17—How was she rewarded?

45. How has today's study helped you form a clearer picture of what holiness is? (Refer to questions 39 and 42.)

46. What are aspects of Elisha's life and the woman's life that you would like to see in your own life? (Before writing an answer, read 1 Cor. 13 and 1 Tim. 6:11.)

[1] *My Utmost for His Highest* by Oswald Chambers. © 1935 by Dodd Mead & Co., renewed © 1963 by the Oswald Chambers Publications Assn. Ltd., and is used by permission of Discovery House Publishers, Box 3566, Grand Rapids, MI 49501. All rights reserved.

[2] J. Sidlow Baxter, *Christian Holiness: Restudies and Restated* (Grand Rapids, Michigan: Zondervan Publishing House, 1977), 112-113.

[3] W. Ian Thomas, *The Mystery of Godliness* (Grand Rapids, Michigan: Zondervan Publishing House, 1964), 17.

[4] Reprinted from *The Pursuit of Holiness*. © 1978 by Jerry Bridges. Used by permission of NavPress, Colorado Springs, CO. All rights reserved.

[5] Sinclair B. Ferguson, *A Heart for God* (Colorado Springs, Colorado: Navpress, 1985), 129. Used by permission.

[6] Max Lucado, *He Still Moves Stones* (Dallas: Word Publishing, 1993), 107. Used by permission.

[7] A. W. Tozer, *The Root of Righteousness* (Camp Hill, Pennsylvania: Christian Publications, 1955, 1986), 25.

WEEK 6
A LOVE FOR GOD'S WORD

DAY 1

1. Write some of your favorite foods in the space below.

2. Why did these foods become your favorites? (check one)

_____ Because they were my best friend's favorites.

_____ Because I liked the pictures of them in advertisements and cookbooks.

_____ Because I like the package they come in.

_____ Because I like the way they taste.

3. Considering what you checked, how does someone get the most enjoyment out of food?

Read Jeremiah 15:16.

4. "Thy words were found and I ate them." At first glance, this phrase seems rather odd. Perhaps if only one word were changed it would make more sense. For instance, "Thy words were found and I heard them." Unless a person is hearing impaired, though, anyone can hear words. But not everyone eats them. Not everyone digests them. Read Jeremiah's phrase again in your Bible. What do you think it indicates about his own commitment to the Word of God, and his love for it?

5. "And Thy words became for me a joy and the delight of my heart." When do you think the Word of God becomes the delight and joy of a person's heart? (Refer to question 2.)

6. What can you learn about a person from what he or she enjoys reading?

"If it is true that a man is known by the company he keeps, it is no less true that his character is reflected in the books he reads, for they are the outward expression of his inner hungers and aspirations."[1] —J. Oswald Sanders

7. According to the last half of the verse, what inclined Jeremiah's heart to love the Word in the first place?

SCRIPTURE MEMORY
A Love For God's Word
■ Job 23:12
■ Psalm 119:165
■ Jeremiah 15:16

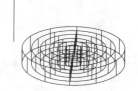

8. And how do you relate to this?

You can almost see the sparkle in Jeremiah's eye and the bounce in his step as he writes about the Word of God. Unfortunately, this is not the experience of every believer in his or her relationship to the Scriptures. Too often this relationship is portrayed as one of sheer drudgery.

Tomorrow we will dissolve this concept as we continue to gain a tender devotion for the Word.

DAY 2

Read 1 John 5:3.

9. "And His commandments are not burdensome." Why are we sometimes deceived into thinking that the opposite is true, that His commandments are a burden?

10. Do you think John is saying here that God's commandments are easy? Why?

11. From memory, write the verse you memorized on "holiness."

12. Are His commandments burdensome to the believer who desires holiness? Why or why not?

13. Are His commandments burdensome to the believer who desires Christlikeness? Why or why not?

14. In what ways do you think Christians convey to each other and to the world that His commandments are burdensome?

15. How is not keeping the commandments the real burden?

16. What could we conclude about someone who claimed to love the Word of God, but who never obeyed what it said?

"If you love Me, you will keep My commandments" (John 14:15).

17. "For this is the love of God." The Bible makes it clear that God's love for us is not based on our performance, but upon Himself. His love is unconditional. (See Titus 3:4-5.) These are the facts. Yet, how do you

think our obedience to His commandments impacts our experience of His love—our assurance of His love?

DAY 3

Read Psalm 19:7-11.

18. Too often we take the Bible for granted. We leave it on a book shelf, in a drawer, on the dresser, in the car, or at the church. Maybe you can remember a time in your life when weeks or even months passed without a single thought about God's Word. But imagine that God had not given us the Bible. Suppose that He withheld His Word from us. He could have. What do you think the world would be like without it?

19. How does today's passage indicate that the Bible will. . .

    a. resuscitate the weary one? (v. 7)

    b. fashion a genius from a fool? (v. 7)

    c. exhilarate the innermost being? (v. 8)

    d. enable the eye to see? (v. 8)

20. Which of the above do you need most right now? Explain. (If you're not certain, think about "d.")

21. Verses 7-9—How are the laws, guidelines, and judgments of the Lord described in these verses?

    Why do you think they are worthy of such descriptions?

22. It may be rather frustrating to try and understand all of the laws and guidelines of the land. The rules that govern society change every day. With this in mind, how do you see the laws of our judicial system as compared with the judgments of the Lord? (Come up with your own observations, but also refer to v. 7-9.)

23. Verse 10—What do you understand about the Bible from the comparisons here?

24. From memory, write the verse you memorized on "temptation."

J. Wallace Hamilton writes, "Western man with all his fine ideals, his social conscience and his multitude of books must rediscover the great Book that he has let slip so carelessly out of his hands. He must find the truth again. He must face the facts again. He must make his way back through all the maze of false ideas that have betrayed him to the message of redemption in the New Testament he has scorned. This Book has the truth about life."[2]

25. Verse 11—According to this verse, how is the Bible profitable for resisting temptation?

How is it profitable for the one who endures?

DAY 4

Read Psalm 119:19-20.

"For indeed in this house we groan, longing to be clothed with our dwelling from heaven" (2 Cor. 5:2).

26. Psalm 119:19—What does the psalmist say here to indicate that he was homesick?

27. When you are away and missing home, a symbol of home can bring great comfort. What was the symbol of home that brought comfort to the psalmist in today's passage?

28. How do you think this reminded him of his true home?

Read Psalm 119:47-48.

29. Verse 48—What does the object of the psalmist's reach indicate about his heart?

30. Verses 47-48—What words are used to describe the psalmist's passion for God's commandments?

31. What impressions would you have about a person who claimed such a passion?

Are you drawn to such a person? Why or why not?

Read Psalm 119:131.

32. What does the psalmist's word picture in this verse teach you about loving the Word?

33. When do you have such a longing for the Word of God?

Read Psalm 119:147-148.

34. When the day's expectations have not yet begun (morning) and when they have been accomplished (evening), for what does the psalmist make time?

35. What does he say to indicate that this is not just another chore to add to his list?

36. With a beginning and ending the way the psalmist describes here, how do you think he fills in the rest of the day?

37. How would you like to relate more to the psalmist and his beliefs?

Read Psalm 119:165.

38. What is true about the person who loves the Word?

Are you drawn to such a person? Why or why not? (Refer to question 31.)

DAY 5

Read Job 23:12.

    a. "You have just won $1,000,000."
    b. "Will you marry me?"
    c. "The job is yours."

39. Imagine that the above statements were directed toward you. If you were to take them seriously, you would have to consider the source of them. When would you be glad to hear them and when would you be repulsed? When would you be suspicious? When would they represent a dream come true, and when would they rain on your parade? In the space below, come up with a couple of possibilities as sources for each statement and write how your reaction would be different depending upon who said it.

statement a.

statement b.

statement c.

> "If there is no passion to learn and apply the Word, no desire to discover what the Word says about the situations we face, we will become malnourished and emaciated and unable to handle trials when they come."[4]
> —Tony Evans

"The command of His lips" (Job 23:12)
"The words of His mouth" (Job 23:12)
"All Scripture is God-breathed" (2 Tim. 3:16).[5]

40. Record your thoughts about the Bible as you meditate upon the truth that every word comes from the mouth of God—that the breath of God still lingers on every word.

41. How seriously can you take the Words of God? Why?

42. In what specific situations do you find it the most difficult to trust the Bible's counsel? Why?

43. Perhaps Job had also been tempted not to trust God, yet what was he able to say in the first part of Job 23:12?

44. What impresses you about his statement in the last half of the verse?

45. Complete this phrase with your own comparison: I have treasured the words of His mouth more than. . .

46. How has this week's study helped you gain a love for God's Word?

[1] Taken from: *Spiritual Leadership* by J. Oswald Sanders. Copyright 1967, Moody Bible Institute of Chicago. Moody Press. Used by permission
[2] J. Wallace Hamilton, *Horns and Halos* (Old Tappan, New Jersey: Fleming H. Revell Company, 1965), 64.
[3] Walter A. Henrichsen, *Many Aspire Few Attain* (Colorado Springs, Colorado: Navpress), 15.
[4] Tony Evans, *Returning to Your First Love* (Chicago: Moody Press, 1995), 41. Used by permission.
[5] *The Student Bible, New International Version* (Grand Rapids, Michigan: Zondervan Bible publishers, 1986).

WEEK 7
RENEWING YOUR MIND

DAY 1

Christlikeness relates to the inner person as well as the outward. We have studied how God has called us to be holy. He desires this of the whole man or woman. At first glance it may seem as though sins of the mind are less harmful than sinful actions. But sin is always sin, and every sin begins in the mind.

"Every sinful act is committed twice: once in our heads and once in our behavior. To win the behavior battle, we must first win the battle that takes place in our minds."[1] —Charles Stanley

"The mind has always been more important to God than our outward actions."[2] —T. W. Hunt

Read Romans 12:1-2.

1. How does verse 1 express the goals of Christlikeness?

2. Verse 2—According to this verse, what hinders these goals from being realized?

3. What type of thoughts do you think are in conformity to the world?

4. Verse 2—Why do you think that Paul points to the mind as the place where transformation begins?

5. Verse 2—What is the transformed mind able to understand?

6. From memory, write the verse you memorized on "a love for God's Word."

7. How does Christ renew your mind through His Word?

SCRIPTURE MEMORY
Thought Life
■ **Romans 12:1-2**
■ **Philippians 4:8**
■ **Colossians 3:2**

> "The opposite of will is instinct (by instinct I mean unwilled reactions). Major or life-changing decisions are not a problem with animals. With human beings, the will is that part of our mind over which we have control. . . . The will enables us to obey in spite of feeling. Often we cannot control our emotions, but we always have control over the will. Our identification with Christ must begin here or not at all."[4]
> —T. W. Hunt

> "The key method Paul underscores as the means of the transformed life is by the 'renewal of the mind.' This means nothing more and nothing less than education. Serious education. In-depth education. Disciplined education in the things of God. It calls for a mastery of the Word of God. We need to be people whose lives have changed because our minds have changed."[3] —R. C. Sproul

DAY 2

Read Colossians 3:1-4.

8. From memory, write the verse you memorized on "who you are in Christ."

9. What are the facts concerning who you are in Christ in regard to. . .

   a. His resurrection (v. 1)

   b. your position (v. 3)

   c. the future (v. 4)

10. If your life is "hidden with Christ in God" (v. 3), then where are you? (see v. 1)

11. Imagine you are in this place physically right now. From this position, what impressions do you have in regard to the cares of the world?

   How does this position help you understand the value of heavenly things?

12. How does this position help you to understand what Paul meant in verse 2?

13. How do you think a person's thought life helps or hinders his or her pursuit of Christlikeness?

14. Re-read verse 2. In today's society, how does a Christian accomplish this?

15. Circle the words or phrases which apply to you regarding the following statement:
   Centering my thoughts on things above is. . .

a chore	a delight	unnatural	too extreme
easy	too serious	impractical	idealistic
a retreat	boring	a joy	

Explain your selection(s).

16. Why must we think of heavenly things in relation to the here and now and not only to the hereafter?

DAY 3

The mind is always active. In slumber, our dreams reveal the potential of our imagination and brain power. When awake, our minds can carry us to exotic places half way around the world, even as our physical bodies occupy a desk at school. In a moment's time our thoughts can run the gamut on topics, as one subject leads us to think of another. What Lois Mowday writes in *The Snare* is true: "We live much of our lives in our minds."[5]

Our thoughts may seem harmless. We have been taught to keep them to ourselves. We have heard, "If you can't say anything nice, don't say anything at all." The truth is, we have an all-knowing Father who hears every thought.

"For the Lord searches all hearts and understands every intent of the thoughts" (1 Chron. 28:9).

Maybe we should go a step further and live by a new principle. "If you can't think anything nice, change your thought patterns." Today's passage continues to focus on the life we live in our minds.

Read Romans 8:5-7.

17. Verse 5—What are the results of the mind set on the flesh?

18. Verse 5—What are the results of the mind set on the Holy Spirit? (Read Gal. 5:22-23.)

19. Verse 6—According to this verse, what words indicate that a person's mindset is a matter of his or her own choice?

20. Verse 6—Why is the thought life such a serious issue?

"To speculate about something is to develop a mental scenario about it. It is to daydream or fantasize about it. Speculations begin with thoughts like. . .
I wonder what would happen if. . .
I wonder what it would be like if. . .
If I only had. . .
If she hadn't. . .
To. . .envision yourself telling someone off and winning the respect of others in doing so is to deceive yourself. To rehearse in your mind imaginary conversations in which you emotionally slam-dunk another person is to

meditate on sin. To mentally devise a scheme where you are benefitted at the expense of someone else is to walk after the flesh."[6] —Charles Stanley

21. Verse 7, "The mind set on the flesh is hostile toward God." Why must we see this as a serious warning?

22. Verse 7—According to the last half of this verse, what is the mind set on the flesh unable to do? (Compare with question 5.)

23. How can you choose to set your mind on the Spirit today?

DAY 4

24. In reference to today's weather, imagine that person A says, "It is partly cloudy"; while person B says, "It is partly sunny." Based upon these statements, write a brief but revealing description of these two people.

Person A:

Person B:

Read Titus 1:15-16.

These verses are written in regard to the Cretan false teachers. In the context of this passage, they are written in reference to unbelievers. But the principles of these verses apply across the board to the Christian and non-Christian alike. And as we shall see, today's passage is very helpful in exposing more symptoms of an unhealthy thought life.

25. Verse 15—How does Paul describe the person with impure thought patterns?

26. Verse 15—How is the defiled and unbelieving heart defective in discerning right from wrong?

27. Verse 16—How is a corrupted mind and conscience exposed outwardly?

"'Even so, every good tree bears good fruit; but the bad tree bears bad fruit. A good tree cannot produce bad fruit, nor can a bad tree produce good fruit'" (Matt. 7:17-18).

28. The fruit of a tree tells the story of what is going on in the hidden life of the tree. Likewise, what do our words and deeds "tell" about the authenticity of our inward Christian life?

29. Based upon today's passage, will an impure person focus on purity? Will a pure person focus on impurity? Explain.

"A person who is pure of heart sees goodness and purity in everything; but a person whose own heart is evil and untrusting finds evil in everything. For his dirty mind and rebellious heart color all he sees and hears" (Titus 1:15).[7]

30. Wayne has made both of the statements below. In light of today's passage, check which one is most revealing about his Christian walk. Explain.

_____ "I am a Christian and I have placed Christ as the number one priority in my life."

_____ "I know that Brian claims to be a good Christian, but it's obvious that his motives are only self serving."

Are you more apt to see the negative aspects in someone rather than the positive? Are you suspicious of peoples' motives? Are you quick to judge? To the defiled and unbelieving nothing is pure. Perhaps it is not so much others who are in need of change.

31. How is the recognition of your own impurities the best way to deal with impurities in someone else?

"Behold, I send you out as sheep in the midst of wolves; therefore be shrewd as serpents, and innocent as doves'" (Matt. 10:16).

32. Concerning the actions and motives of others, what do you think is the difference between being pure and being naive?

How has today's study exposed unhealthy thought patterns in your life? Go ahead and give these to God. He knows about them already. But He also loves you enough to expose them to you. This is what has happened today. Remember, His desire is to make you holy, not to make you feel guilty.

DAY 5

Read Jeremiah 4:14.

33. What form of evil is Jeremiah referring to in the last half of this verse?

"Wash your heart from evil, O Jerusalem, that you may be saved. How long will your wicked thoughts lodge within you?" (Jere. 4:14).

34. When do you think wicked thoughts become fixed in the heart?

35. We would like to think that, when our senses are exposed to the evil around us, our hearts will remain numb to it: unaffected. Is this being realistic or naive? Explain.

36. We may have the appearance of outward cleanliness in our conduct, but how does this verse indicate that it is the inner person needing the bath?

We may think that putting aside the evil influences in our lives is enough to bathe our hearts. Physically, it is never enough just to remove ourselves from the mud. If we want to be clean, we must lather up the soap. This is also true in regard to our spiritual lives. Remember, the believer's life is not only characterized by removing the old. It also consists of taking in the new. Our hearts must be immersed in the things of God.

Read Philippians 4:8.

37. Why could the virtues listed in this verse cause you to think of God?

38. How can you think on these things in the face of corruption and vulgarism in the world today?

39. How does this verse indicate that such thinking is an act of the will?

40. How do your choices in regard to the following impact your thoughts of God? Rate each one a scale from 1 to 5. Five represents a strong encouragement to meditate upon God.

_____A. Friendships	_____F. Movies
_____B. Music	_____G. Goals
_____C. Television	_____H. Job/Occupation
_____D. Magazines	_____I. Leisure time
_____E. Books	_____J. Conversations

41. Of the things you listed a 1, 2, or 3, do you think they are damaging to a godly life? Explain. (Refer to question 35.)

42. List specific influences in your life that cause your mind to "think on these things," the things listed in Philippians 4:8.

43. Look again at question 40. Which one(s) is God impressing upon you to change?

How does this call you to action?

44. No one else can know your thoughts. No one else knows how something influences your thinking. This is something only you and God know. What are some things you can think of that will give accountability to your thought life, that will hold your thoughts in check?

[1] Charles Stanley, *The Wonderful Spirit Filled Life* (Nashville: Thomas Nelson, 1992), 91.

[2] T. W. Hunt, *The Mind of Christ* (Nashville: Broadman & Holman Publishers, 1995), 4.

[3] R. C. Sproul, *The Holiness of God* (Wheaton, Illinois: Tyndale House Publishers, 1985), 210.

[4] Hunt, *The Mind of Christ*, 13.

[5] Lois Mowday, *The Snare* (Colorado Springs: Navpress, 1988), 91-92.

[6] Stanley, *The Wonderful Spirit Filled Life*, 93.

[7] *The Living Bible* (Wheaton, Illinois: Tyndale House Publishers, 1971, 1973).

[8] *My Utmost for His Highest* by Oswald Chambers. © 1935 by Dodd Mead & Co., renewed © 1963 by the Oswald Chambers Publications Assn. Ltd., and is used by permission of Discovery House Publishers, Box 3566, Grand Rapids, MI 49501. All rights reserved.

WEEK 8
MOTIVES OF THE HEART

SCRIPTURE MEMORY
Motives
- ■ Proverbs 16:2
- ■ Matthew 6:1
- ■ 1 Corinthians 10:31

DAY 1

"All the ways of a man are clean in his own sight, but the Lord weighs the motives" (Prov. 16:2).

"Does He not consider it who weighs the hearts? And does He not know it who keeps your soul?" (Prov. 24:12).

"For Thou alone dost know the hearts of the sons of men" (2 Chron. 6:30).

In His master plan, God is creating us after His likeness. It is a work He begins in the believer's life the moment the new birth occurs. At that moment, His life indwells the new Christian. His intentions are to re-create the heart. It is the heart that influences the believer's every action. These heart influences are motives, the focus of our study this week.

Read 1 Corinthians 4:2-5.

1. Verse 2—According to this verse, what is the requirement of a steward or servant of Christ?

2. Verses 3-4—Was Paul convinced that he was living up to this requirement when the church members considered it so?_____
When the other apostles evaluated him?_____
When his own conscience declared it to be true?_____

3. Verse 4—Whose judgment carried the weight in terms of Paul's success as a servant of Christ?

4. Verse 5—According to the last half of this verse, on what basis is this judgment carried out?

5. Verse 5—Good deeds done in the name of religion may produce no eternal reward. On the other hand, deeds which produce little human

approval may receive the praise of God. Is it our hands or our hearts that determine the value of our actions before God? Why?

"Many a solo is sung to show off; many a sermon is preached as an exhibition of talent; many a church is founded as a slap at some other church. . .in the sight of God we are judged not so much by what we do as by our reasons for doing it. Not what but why will be the important question when we Christians appear at the judgment seat to give account of the deeds done in the body."[1]
—A. W. Tozer

6. Verse 5—What does this verse teach you about God?

7. How do you think your life would be impacted if you lived every day remembering that Christ is your Judge?

8. Verse 5—According to this verse, in what area are we to be content being left in the "dark"? Why?

9. How do you think you can know when your motives are right?

"Unfortunately, too often our motives are self-centered rather than God-centered. We want to maintain our reputation before others, or we want to feel good about ourselves. Or we may even seek to live a decent and moral life or to do good deeds because such an ethic has been instilled in us from childhood. But that motivation is never related to God and thus is not acceptable to Him."[2] —Jerry Bridges

DAY 2

The Scriptures are specific in revealing impure motives, but they also provide some biblical "measuring sticks" to help us determine when our motives are right. Today's verses give us a divine assessment of when our motives please God.

Read 1 Corinthians 10:31.

10. What does this verse state is the correct motive for whatever you do?

11. "Whether, then, you eat or drink." How is it possible to glorify God in things that, at first glance, don't seem like spiritual things, that may not seem to relate to Him at all?

12. "Whether, then, you eat or drink." What impact can the right motives have on the person performing basic, daily activities?

Read Colossians 3:17.

13. If a word or deed is performed in the name of Jesus, how should that obligate a person to speak or act?

14. As a Christian, is there anything you do that does not bear His name? Explain.

15. "Giving thanks through Him to God the Father." How do you think a thankful heart will help motivate and energize our actions?

Read 1 Peter 4:11.

16. What should be the single reason for all that we do? (Compare with question 10.)

17. How does this motive take good deeds and turn them into godly deeds?

18. What is the difference between performing a deed in your own strength and performing it in the strength of the Lord?

DAY 3

Read Matthew 6:1-8.

19. Verses 1, 2, 5—According to these verses, what motivates the hypocrite?

20. " 'They have their reward in full.' " Does the hypocrite get the reward he or she desires? Explain.

21. Verse 1—Yet what is lacking in this reward?

22. How do you think we are tempted to sound the trumpet today in regard to the acts of charity that we do?

23. Verse 5—According to this verse, when do our motives put our prayer life on the street corner?

24. Verse 7—In this verse, what does Jesus teach about motives relating to prayer?

25. When do you think our prayer requests reveal impure motives?

26. From memory, write the verse you memorized on "temptation."

27. Verses 3, 4, 6—What does Jesus recommend to head off the temptation of impure motives?

   Why do you think this is effective?

28. Verse 6—What is the reward of secret actions performed from the right motives?

29. Write something good that you have done in the past week.

30. What motives could have made this deed even better?

"It is so important to make Jesus our Lord from a motive to please him and not to get something from him. We must give him our businesses, our families and our relationships to bring joy to his heart."[3]
—Floyd McClung

DAY 4

Read Matthew 23:25-28.

31. Why were the Pharisees rejected by Jesus?

32. Verses 25-26—In these verses, what do Jesus' comparisons teach you about the importance of motives?

33. You do not produce a clean cup by pouring a new beverage in it. Not only will the cup remain dirty, but it will also contaminate the new liquid inside. What spiritual principles can we learn from this as well?

34. Verse 26—Notice the principle in this verse. How do you think a pure heart will inevitably be confirmed in the outer person?

35. No matter how beautifully a coffin is designed and adorned, it still has the character of death: the feeling of death, the presence of death, the essence of death. When does the believer's life take on

the character of an adorned coffin?

36. Read this list of words: envy, jealousy, sensuality, spite, revenge, pride, greed, guilt. How are believers motivated by such impulses?

37. What is the tragedy of a believer giving into such impulses? (Refer to question 35.)

"As water cannot rise higher than its source, so the moral quality in an act can never be higher than the motive that inspires it. For this reason no act that arises from an evil motive can be good, even though some good may appear to come out of it. Every deed done out of anger or spite for instance will be found to have been done for the enemy and against the kingdom of God."[4]
—A. W. Tozer

38. This week, we have learned that while man looks at the outward appearances, God looks at the heart. What do we communicate to the all-knowing God when we take on the attitude that we couldn't care less about our evil motives and continue focusing on impressing people?

39. After thinking through question 38, what do you want to communicate to God right now? Write it below.

40. How might the choices below be the difference between one who is led or motivated and one who is driven?

   a. Living to glorify God
   b. Living to impress people

DAY 5

Read James 2:1-9.

41. Verses 1-3—Think about a modern-day version of the scenario in these verses and write it below.

42. Verse 4—"Have you not. . .become judges with evil motives?" What do you think would motivate such actions as you described above?

43. Verses 3 and 6—How do poor people become victims of wrong motives?

44. In verse 9, how does James describe such actions as you listed in question 43?

45. How might evil motives impact a person's choice of friends? (Refer to your answers from question 42.)

46. Would you want to be chosen as a friend on the basis of such motives? Why or why not? (Come up with your own reasons, but also refer to verses 6-7.)

47. Verse 8—What is a healthy motive in regard to relationships?

48. Why could you trust friends who were motivated to befriend you on this basis?

49. Think about these words from today's passage:
    personal favoritism   special attention
    distinctions   partiality

    These describe the actions of verses 1-3. What type of people are we tempted to treat with such superiority? Why?

Maybe you look at this and think, "There are worse things a person could do. It is simply the way of life. If you want to get ahead you have to associate with and impress the right people. After all, it's not really what you know but who you know. If you want to win the game of life, you have to play by its rules."

But are we really at the world's mercy? Are we helpless to what it dictates? Or do we simply hide behind such excuses so that we can pursue our own desires, our own agendas, our own plans. Could it be that we have surrendered to the tempter in an area where Jesus stood firm?

"Again, the devil took Him to a very high mountain, and showed Him all the kingdoms of the world, and their glory; and he said to Him, 'All these things will I give You, if You fall down and worship me'" (Matt. 4:8-9).

What motivates you? Your reasons for relating with people will tell you a lot. Is it the desires of the flesh or is it Christ's likeness that motivates you? If you have determined to make godliness your goal, you cannot brush aside motives as though they have no significance—motives which James describes as evil in verse 4.

50. From memory, write the verse you memorized on "the believer's life."

51. Write the name of a person you know at church or school who is not respected by other people.

What is the potential of this person? (Refer to question 50 and Jas. 2:5.)

52. What actions has today's study motivated you to do in regard to this person?

[1] A.W. Tozer, *The Root of the Righteous* (Camp Hill, Pennsylvania: Christian Publications, 1955, 1986), 91.

[2] Jerry Bridges, *The Practice of Godliness* (Colorado Springs: Navpress, 1983), 71.

[3] Taken from *Basic Discipleship* by Floyd McClung. © 1988, 1990 by Floyd McClung. Used with permission from Inter-Varsity Press, P.O. Box 1400, Downers Grove, IL 60515.

[4] Tozer, *The Root of the Righteous*, 89.

WEEK 9
WHOLEHEARTEDNESS

DAY 1

The word *wholeheartedness* leaves no stone unturned, so to speak. It brings to mind a sense of thoroughness. But wholeheartedness also relates to an attitude of enthusiasm with which a thorough job is completed. We will begin this week's study by looking at wholeheartedness in our relationship with God.

SCRIPTURE MEMORY
Wholeheartedness
■ Deuteronomy 4:29
■ 2 Chronicles 16:9
■ Colossians 3:23

1. **2 Chronicles 16:9a—According to this verse, what is the longing of God's heart?**

2. **"Whose heart is completely His"—What do you think it means in the life of a person when God has complete ownership of his or her heart?**

3. **Jeremiah 24:7—" ' "I will give them a heart to know Me." ' " When did God give you a heart to know Him?**

4. **According to this verse, what is true about the person whose heart belongs to God?**

5. **" ' "For they will return to Me with their whole heart." ' " What issues in your life prevent your being wholehearted in your personal relationship with God?**

"Long ago I came to the conclusion that if Jesus Christ is not controlling all of me, the chances are very good that He is not controlling any of me. . .Jesus Christ wants to be and must be Lord. He must be head of and lord of all departments of our lives. We cannot have a girlfriend or a husband or a home or a job shut up in an airtight compartment that Jesus cannot control."[1]
—A. W. Tozer

6. **What role do feelings play in regard to a person's willingness to respond to God wholeheartedly?**

7. **Deuteronomy 4:29—According to this verse, which comes first, the sense of God's presence or a wholehearted search for Him?**

> "As long as Jesus is one of many options, he is no option. As long as you can carry your burdens alone, you don't need a burden bearer. As long as your situation brings you no grief, you will receive no comfort. And as long as you can take him or leave him, you might as well leave him, because he won't be taken halfheartedly."[2]
> —Max Lucado

8. So in light of your answer on question 7, how might this verse counsel the person who is apathetic or emotionless in his or her walk with God?

9. After today's study, how is God specifically leading you out of apathy and into a wholehearted commitment to Him?

DAY 2

As we seek to become wholehearted in our relationship to God, He will strengthen our character with wholeheartedness in other areas. Today we will look at how wholehearted love for God impacted specific people in the Scriptures and in turn, how their lives may have impacted others.

- **The Example of Jesus**

10. Mark 7:37—According to the last half of this verse, what specific miracles impressed the multitudes?

11. " 'He has done all things well.' " How does this phrase relate to wholeheartedness?

12. How do you think Jesus may have specifically manifested wholehearted love for God in the following areas? Remember, He did all things well.

   A. In His teaching

   B. In His carpentry work

   C. In His personal disciplines

13. John 17:4—What was He able to say before He died?

- **The Example of Joshua**

Joshua's life is often overshadowed by the greatness of the events and people that surrounded him. Yet his usefulness to God is undeniable. The following verse will help us see the truth of this and will allow us to discover more dimensions of wholeheartedness.

14. Joshua 11:15—What can a person learn about wholeheartedness by observing Joshua's life?

15. How did Joshua take personally what the Lord had entrusted to Moses?

16. How do you think this impacted his work?

17. As you consider this verse, how do you think Joshua responded in the following situations. . .

   A. When a task was delegated to him?

   B. When someone else received the credit for something he did?

   C. When he was not pampered with encouragement or attention?

18. Why do you think Joshua would be an asset to a team or class project?

- **The Example of Paul**

19. 2 Timothy 4:7—What was Paul able to say before he died?

20. What issues of wholeheartedness do you see in this passage?

21. How do you think Paul responded. . .

   . . .when everyone else lacked motivation and enthusiasm in their walk with God?

   . . .in his trade as a tentmaker? (See Acts 18:1-3.)

22. Read 2 Timothy 4:8—What motivated Paul in his wholehearted efforts?

23. From memory, write the verse you memorized on "a love for God's Word."

24. When you consider the contribution Paul made to the New Testament, how do you think his writings reflect wholeheartedness?

"Few indeed are the people who finish what they start—and do a complete job of it. . . The rare but beautiful experience of carrying out a responsibility to its completion. . .When you have accomplished or thoroughly fulfilled a task, there is a feeling of satisfaction that cannot be expressed in words. . . So what are you waiting for? Does it need painting? Paint it—and do a thorough job! Does it need cleaning? Clean it—thoroughly! Does it need ironing? Iron it—wrinkle free, with gusto! Does it need attention? Give it thorough, unrestrained attention! Stop being satisfied with a halfhearted, incomplete job! Stun those around you with a thorough, finished product! AND STOP PUTTING IT OFF!"[3]
—Charles Swindoll

25. How has your life been impacted by his wholehearted approach? (Refer to question 24.)

• The Example of Philemon

26. Philemon 21—What was Paul able to say about Philemon?

27. What aspects of wholeheartedness do you see in this?

28. What might impress you about Philemon?

29. Consider questions 11, 12, 20, 21, 27, and 28. What does wholeheartedness look like?

DAY 3

30. When you hear that someone has poured his or her heart into a task, what do you understand this to mean?

31. What risks do you think people take when they pour their heart into their work. . .

   . . .merely to please others?

   . . .merely to please self?

Read Colossians 3:22-24.

32. Verse 22—To whom does Paul address these words?

33. Verse 22—"masters on earth." List some people in your life whose positions give them authority over you.

34. What energy level do you pour into accomplishing their requests when they are watching you as compared to when they are not?

"Obey. . .not only when their eye is on you and to win their favor" (Col. 3:22, NIV).

35. From memory, write the verse you memorized on "motives."

36. Verse 23—What should be the real motive for Christians behind any job or task we accomplish, no matter who asks us to do it?

37. When motivated this way, why is any task you accomplish worthy of a wholehearted effort? (Compare with question 31.)

38. Verse 24—How can earthly occupations produce eternal rewards?

"God makes no distinction between what is religious and what is secular. We are to consider Him our employer regardless of our place of employment. Just as our earthly employees pay us a wage, Paul said God will as well. Paul went so far as to say that our eternal reward is in some way tied to our performance on our jobs."[5] —Charles Stanley

39. How does wholeheartedness in a particular task relate to your sense of accomplishment in that task?

40. When you consider Paul's instruction in today's passage, do you think he would ever label any task a "waste of time"? Explain.

DAY 4

"He also who is slack in his work is brother to him who destroys" (Prov. 18:9).

As we continue our study of wholeheartedness, we will observe the flip side of the coin in the life of King Saul. His life is an example of how halfhearted obedience results in tragedy.

Read 1 Samuel 15:1-35.

41. Verse 3—What did God specifically instruct King Saul to do?

42. Verses 7-8—How did he obey?

43. Verse 9—Yet, how did he disobey?

44. Verses 10-21—How did God view Saul's deeds?

45. Verses 22-23—What does this teach you about God?

46. Verse 24—According to Saul, what was the reason for his halfhearted obedience?

"To wash feet may be the job of slaves, but to wash His feet is royal work. To loosen shoe strings is terrible employment, but to loosen the great Master's shoes is a royal privilege. The barn, the shop, and the factory all become temples when men and women do all to the glory of God. The divine service is not a thing of a few hours and a few places, but all of life becomes holiness unto the Lord, and every place and thing is as consecrated as the tabernacle and its golden candlestick."[6] —Charles H. Spurgeon

47. Verse 28—What was the consequence of Saul's sin?

48. What does today's passage teach you in regard to wholehearted obedience in your own life?

We will be wise to grasp another lesson regarding wholeheartedness from this passage. It relates to wholeheartedly seeking the Lord's will rather than wholeheartedly seeking our own will.

"'I regret that I have made Saul King'" (v. 11).
"The Glory of Israel . . . is not a man that He should change His mind" (v. 29).
"And the Lord regretted that He had made Saul king over Israel" (v. 35).

At first glance these phrases may seem to contradict each other. In fact, if we just look at the surface, they may seem to contradict the very nature of God. If God doesn't change His mind, how could He regret making Saul the king over Israel? But we must remember that in His sovereignty, God has given man a free choice. And in regard to Israel, their choice was to have a king. In fact, they prayed for a king.

"But the thing was displeasing in the sight of Samuel when they said, 'Give us a king to judge us.' And Samuel prayed to the Lord. And the Lord said to Samuel, 'Listen to the voice of the people in regard to all that they say to you, for they have not rejected you, but they have rejected Me from being King over them. . . . Now then, listen to their voice; however, you shall solemnly warn them and tell them of the procedure of the king who will reign over them'" (1 Sam. 8:6-7, 9).

As they observed other nations ruled by human kings, their discontentment of an intangible, invisible King grew. They were no longer satisfied with God as their King. So they prayed for a human monarch, and God granted their request. After studying today's passage, we can see that the choice Israel made in desiring a human, tangible king was not the best for them. Yet in His sovereignty, God had determined that Israel would have a free choice. He cannot change His mind in regard to this. So we see the heart of a Father here: regret on behalf of His people in regard to the choice they made to have a human king.

Is it possible that God's regret for us is the same? He observes our choices and the consequences, and He regrets what happens. But He has said in the beginning that we are free to choose, even if our choices break His heart. We have much to learn from this. Perhaps we are too hasty in placing our requests before God: perhaps too specific at times. We ask for things that are not the best for us, just as the nation of Israel did, and sometimes we are granted those things. Could it be that we should have only one request in our wholehearted praying?

"Yet not My will, but Thine be done" (Luke 22:42).

49. Write something specific for which you have been praying.

Why is it best to entrust this to God's will rather than your own?

DAY 5

"So there was great joy in Jerusalem because there was nothing like this in Jerusalem since the days of Solomon the son of David, king of Israel" (2 Chron. 30:26).

The above verse summarizes the welfare of Judah during the reign of king Hezekiah. From the beginning of his rulership, he sought to undo the iniquity of his father, Ahaz, by purifying the temple according to the law of Moses. This restoration carried over into the temple worship and into the celebration of the Passover to which all of Judah and Israel was summoned. Though there are many interesting aspects that occurred here, today we will focus on only two verses that summarize Hezekiah's heart.

Read 2 Chronicles 31:20-21.

50. Verse 21—What aspects of wholeheartedness do you see here?

51. Verse 20—What was the character of his work as described in this verse?

"And every work which he began in the service of the house of God."

52. Answer yes or no. Do you get the idea that Hezekiah. . .
_____ slept through the Sabbath worship services?
_____ grumbled about a lack of appreciation for his work in the Temple?
_____ ever thought, "One 'church' thing a week is enough for me"?
_____ labored in the Temple only when he had leftover time from his other grueling responsibilities as a king?

53. Considering questions 50, 51 and 52, what example does Hezekiah set for us in regard to church participation?

54. How do you think the kingdom of God would benefit if individual church members embraced Hezekiah's example?

55. What do your own answers to question 54 indicate that God may be asking of you?

[1] A. W. Tozer, *Faith Beyond Reason* (Camp Hill, Pennsylvania: Christian Publications, 1989), 58, 60.

[2] Max Lucado, *The Applause of Heaven* (Dallas: Word Publishing, 1990), 56. Used by permission.

[3] Taken from *Devotions for Growing Strong in the Seasons of Life*. Copyright © 1983 by Charles Swindoll, Inc. Used by permission of Zondervan Publishing House.

[4] Charles H. Spurgeon, *Morning and Evening* (Nashville: Thomas Nelson Publishers, 1994), December 11 entry.

[5] Charles Stanley, *The Wonderful Spirit Filled Life* (Nashville: Thomas Nelson, 1992), 140-141.

WEEK 10
HUMILITY

DAY 1

The ego is a demanding thing; it wants whatever will expand its horizons. Oftentimes we Christians find ourselves, along with everyone else, feasting our own egos on some of the world's most enticing rewards, such as acknowledgment, acclaim, and applause. Unfortunately, as we find ourselves in hot pursuit of these things, we distance ourselves more and more from the godly image planned for us from above. For while pride may produce a standing ovation, only humility brings people to their knees.

Read Philippians 2:3-11.

1. From memory, write the verse you memorized on "thought life."

2. What significance do you think a person's thoughts play in relationship to a humble spirit?

3. "But with humility of mind." What type of thoughts do you think consume a humble mind? (Refer to verse 4.)

4. Verse 6—Why did Christ have reason to boast in His ministry here on earth?

5. Verses 7-8—Yet, how does Paul describe Jesus' ministry?

6. What kind of thoughts do you think help to produce such a ministry? (Refer to question 3.)

7. Verses 7-8—What does Jesus' example teach you about humility?

8. "He existed in the form of God." What do Jesus' actions teach you about the "form of God," or in other words, what He is like?

9. "Found in the appearance as a man." What do Jesus' actions in verses

SCRIPTURE MEMORY
Humility
■ Proverbs 22:4
■ Philippians 2:3
■ 1 Peter 5:6

> "Humility is the hallmark of the man whom God can use, although it is not in the world's curriculum. In the realm of politics and commerce, humility is a quality neither coveted nor required. . .But in God's scale of values, humility stands very high."[1]
> —J. Oswald Sanders

7 and 8 teach you about God's dream for humanity?

10. "Did not regard equality with God a thing to be grasped." Yet, how does Christ's humility make it possible for us to know and grasp God?

11. Verses 9-11—How did God respond to Christ's humility?

"Have this attitude in yourselves which was also in Christ Jesus" (Phil. 2:5).

12. How can you take Jesus' examples in regard to humility and apply them to yourself?

"How is it that people who are quite obviously eaten up with Pride can say they believe in God and appear to themselves very religious? I am afraid it means they are worshipping an imaginary God. They theoretically admit themselves to be nothing in the presence of this phantom God, but are really all the time imagining how He approves of them and thinks them far better than ordinary people: that is, they pay a pennyworth of imaginary humility to Him and get out of it a pound's worth of Pride towards their fellow men. . .Whenever we find that our religious life is making us feel that we are good—above all, that we are better than someone else—I think we may be sure that we are being acted on, not by God, but by the devil. The real test of being in the presence of God is that you either forget about yourself altogether or see yourself as a small, dirty object. It is better to forget about yourself altogether."[2]
—C. S. Lewis

DAY 2

Read 1 Peter 5:5-6.

13. "Under the mighty hand of God." Imagine yourself under the mighty hand of God. (That's where you are, you know.) Does this thought give you a sense of claustrophobia? Freedom? Security? Panic? Write how you feel using your own descriptions.

14. Verse 6, "Humble yourselves, therefore, under the mighty hand of God." Humility happily accepts this position. What do you think are characteristics of someone who would not happily accept this position? Explain. (Come up with at least three examples.)

15. How does humility discover the generosity of that same hand? What are the rewards of humility seen in the following verses?

verse 5

verse 6

16. Verse 5—How can the teenage years become humility's finest hour?

17. How does question 16 speak to you personally?

18. Verse 5, "Clothe yourselves with humility toward one another."
Check any of the following that you think would make up a
"wardrobe of humility" in relationship to others.
___Refuses compliments   ___Self-sufficient
___Feels inferior to others   ___Self-conscious
___Childlike   ___Secure and serene
___Despises arrogance in others
___Willingly accepts a lower position than deserved
___Angered or uncomfortable if not the center of attention
___Genuinely interested in others' opinions

19. Why is humility in other people attractive to you?

DAY 3

Today's study focuses on humility in the life of Paul.

20. According to the following verses, what had humility taught Paul
about himself?

1 Corinthians 15:9

Ephesians 3:8

1 Timothy 1:15

21. Do you think his statements in the above verses reveal a healthy or
unhealthy self-image? Explain.

22. "I labored even more than all of them" (1 Cor. 15:10). How might this
sentence be a statement of pride?

23. But look at this phrase in the context of the entire verse. How is it a
statement of humility?

"If you want to find out how proud you are the easiest way is to ask yourself, 'How much do I dislike it when other people snub me, or refuse to take any notice of me, or shove their oar in, or patronize me, or show off?' The point is that each person's pride is in competition with every one else's pride. It is because I wanted to be the big noise at the party that I am so annoyed at someone else being the big noise. . .Pride is essentially competitive."[3]
—C. S. Lewis

24. What are some abilities, attributes, and achievements in your life that could become sources of pride?

25. 1 Corinthians 4:7—How is this verse a "reality check" in regard to the things you wrote about on question 24?

"The humble person is free from pride or arrogance. He submits himself to others and is helpful and courteous. The humble person does not consider himself to be self-sufficient. And yet he recognizes his own gifts, resources, and achievement. He knows that he has been the object of undeserved, redeeming love. Therefore he cannot build up himself for he knows it is 'all of grace.' "[4] —John Edmund Haggai

26. How might another person's success bring our pride to the surface?

27. From memory, write the verse you memorized on "hating sin."

28. Why is pride so difficult to hate?

"The crucible is for silver and the furnace for gold and a man is tested by the praise accorded him" (Prov. 27:21).

29. Imagine that someone has complimented you on a job well done. What do you think could be the best response reflecting true humility?

DAY 4

Read Isaiah 57:15 and Isaiah 66:1-2.

30. Isaiah 57:15a and Isaiah 66:1—What do these verses say about the position of the Lord?

31. Isaiah 66:1-2a—What does a person of humility understand, even as he or she works for the Lord?

32. Why would pride find this (question 31) offensive?

"All of us fall into that self-gratifying pride all the time. It's what we do for God with our strength that becomes important to us. We forget that we could not breathe a breath or think a thought or accomplish anything if it were not for God's moment by moment blessing."[6] —Lloyd John Ogilvie

"A prison of pride is filled with self-made men and women determined to pull themselves up by their own bootstraps even if they land on their rear ends. It doesn't matter what they did or to whom they did it or where they will end up; it only matters that 'I did it my way.' "[7] —Max Lucado

33. From memory, write the verse you memorized on "temptation."

34. How do you think the enemy tempts us with pride in regard to Christian work?

"Too many of us are very humble when there is anything to be done, and never at any other time as far as anybody can see. . .It is unfortunately very frequent amongst professing Christians. Christian humility is not particular about the sort of work it does for Jesus. Never mind whether you are on the quarter-deck, with gold lace on your coat and epaulets on your shoulders as an officer, or whether you are a cabin-boy doing the humblest duties, or a stoker working away down fifty feet below daylight. As long as the work is done for the great Admiral, that is enough."[8] —Alexander Maclaren

35. Isaiah 57:15 and Isaiah 66:2—What words in these verses describe humility?

36. And how is humility rewarded according to these same verses?

37. What are further rewards of humility and/or consequences of pride according to the following verses?

Rewards of humility	Consequences of pride
A. Proverbs 11:2	
B. Matthew 23:12	
C. James 4:6	

"Heaven is My throne" (Isa. 66:1).
"I dwell on a high and holy place" (Isa. 57:15).

38. Imagine the distance between God and man, and yet He desires and seeks a relationship with us. What would happen if our reaching up toward Him were in like proportion?

DAY 5

"Pride runs deep in all of us—pride of race, that makes us despise other nationalities or even other skin colours; pride of class, that keeps us from making friends and showing kindness; pride of intellect, that makes us despise others as fools; pride of denomination, that keeps us apart from other believers; pride of spirituality, that makes us despise even other Christians; pride of subculture or in group towards all those outside of it."[9] —Michael Griffiths

"Pride goes before destruction, and a haughty spirit before stumbling" (Prov. 16:18).

Read Daniel 4:4-37.

39. **Verses 4-7—Why was King Nebuchadnezzar troubled, and what did he do?**

40. **Verses 8-9,18—What had the king observed in Daniel?**

41. **Verse 25—How does Daniel interpret the dream?**

42. **Verse 26—What would happen if the king repented?**

43. **Verse 27—How does Daniel advise him?**

44. **Verse 30—Yet 12 months later (v. 29), how do we see Nebuchadnezzar still caught in the snare of pride?**

45. **Verses 31-33—What happened to him?**

46. **Verse 34—What is the first thing Nebuchadnezzar does here?**

    What is the significance of this in relationship to humility?

47. **Verses 34b-35, 37—What was he able to understand about God?**

48. **Will pride be able to understand such depth (question 47)? Why or why not?**

"The king's pride was to him a kind of insanity which drove him at last into the fields to dwell with the beasts. While he saw himself large and God small he was insane; sanity returned only as he began to see God as all and himself as nothing."[11] —A. W. Tozer

49. How is the Lord using today's study with what is going on in your life right now?

50. How does this call you to action?

[1] Taken from: *Spiritual Leadership* by J. Oswald Sanders. Copyright 1967, Moody Bible Institute of Chicago. Moody Press. Used by permission.

[2] *Mere Christianity* by C. S. Lewis copyright © C. S. Lewis Pte. Ltd. 1942, 1943, 1944, 1952. Extract reprinted by permission.

[3] Ibid., 94-95.

[4] John Edmund Haggai, *Lead On!* (Milton Keynes, England: Word Publishing, 1986), 59. Used by permission.

[5] Elisabeth Elliot, *Discipline, The Glad Surrender* (Old Tappan, New Jersey: Fleming H. Revell Company, 1982), 85.

[6] Lloyd John Ogilvie, *Lord of the Impossible* (Nashville: Abingdon Press, 1984), 23. Used by permission.

[7] Max Lucado, *The Applause of Heaven* (Dallas: Word Publishing, 1990), 52. Used by permission.

[8] Alexander Maclaren, *Exposition of Holy Scripture, Hebrews-1 John* (Grand Rapids, Michigan: Baker Book House, 1974, 1977), 136-137.

[9] Michael Griffiths, *The Example of Jesus* (reproduced by permission of William Neill-Hall Ltd., Cornwall, England), 98. Used by permission.

[10] Lewis, *Mere Christianity*.

[11] A. W. Tozer, *The Divine Conquest* (Urichsville, Ohio: Barbour and Company, 1950), 52.

Do you have what it takes to endure?

WEEK 11
ENDURANCE

DAY 1

Endurance is the stamina of Christian discipleship. It is a word that means to persevere. In modern terms we might refer to it as "stick-to-it-iveness." Endurance traverses the deep rivers, crosses the vast plains, climbs the high mountains. Endurance is the inner strength which does not quit when almost all else says stop. It knows the value of small successes, and positively uses the wisdom which accompanies failure. Endurance has a great reward for those who embody it.

"But the one who endures to the end, he shall be saved" *(Matt. 24:13).*

"Those who can remain. . .are a rare breed. I don't necessarily mean win, I just mean remain. Hang in there. Finish. Stick to it until it is done. But unfortunately, very few of us do that. Our human tendency is to quit too soon. Our human tendency is to stop before we cross the finish line."[1] —Max Lucado

1. 1 Corinthians 15:58—What words in this verse encourage "stick-to-it-iveness?"

2. "Steadfast; immovable." How do you think endurance refuses to budge, even as it abounds in the work of the Lord?

3. If endurance does not see immediate results, will it consider its work a failure? Explain.

4. 1 Corinthians 15:58b—What does the person of endurance remember about all work of the Lord?

5. Galatians 6:9—When do you think Christians are tempted to become weary in doing good?

6. If a person is to endure in doing good, what must he or she remember?

How does this motivate you in doing good?

7. **It is easy to relate endurance to activity, in completing a task, for example. But why do you think endurance is useful in waiting or being still?**

8. **Isaiah 40:31—What is produced from the endurance of waiting?**

9. **How could you benefit from this form of endurance (question 8) right now?**

Sometimes when we read the words of those
who have been more
than conquerors, we feel almost despondent.

I feel that I shall never be like that.

But they won through step by step
    by little bits of wills
    little denials of self
    little inward victories
    by faithfulness in very little things.

They became what they are. No one sees
these little hidden steps. They only see
the accomplishment, but even so, those small
steps were taken.

There is no sudden triumph
    no spiritual maturity
That is the work of the moment.[2]

—Amy Carmichael

DAY 2

Read Hebrews 12:1-3.

10. **"Run with endurance the race." What can the endurance of a physical race teach you about the endurance of the spiritual race?**

11. **"Also lay aside every encumbrance, and the sin which so easily entangles us." What are things that might slow down the runner in a physical race?**

> "As the image of the race used by the writer to the Hebrews suggests, this is not merely the passive waiting at the bus-stop, but rather the active endurance of the marathon. It is not achieved by the brief effort of a moment, but by sustained and continual looking to Jesus as our example."[3]
> —Michael Griffiths

12. **When would the following become an encumbrance: something that weights down or slows down the runner of the spiritual race?**

    a. Attitudes

    b. Dating choices

    c. Friendships

    d. Laziness

    e. Priorities

13. **What do you think are some of the sins that most often "entangle" your peers, preventing them from running the race with endurance? Why?**

14. **From memory, write the verse you memorized on "wholeheartedness."**

15. **How might wholeheartedness help free us from the encumbrances (question 12) and the sins (question 13) that so easily entangle us?**

16. **"Therefore, since we have so great a cloud of witnesses surrounding us." These "witnesses" relate to the specific people written about in chapter 11 who have preceded us in the race of endurance. This chapter is referred to often as "the hall of faith." We also have people today who are watching us as we run the race: Christians and non-Christians alike. And though others may observe us, on what must we keep a sharp focus? (Heb. 12:2)**

17. **Why is this so important if we are to run the race with endurance?**

18. **Verses 2-3—What can we learn about endurance from what Jesus modeled?**

"Endurance may be a gift of God, or it may be a counterfeit. Some people are just too lazy to react; others may be so proud that they will not dignify their attackers with a response. Some of us are by nature more insensitive to criticism than others and hence have an appearance of long-suffering. Some by ordinary human calculation will endure a temporary hardship to gain a long-range advantage.

What we must emphasize here is the Source of the long-suffering and the motive for it. It is what makes people endure that counts."[4] —John W. Sanderson

19. "The author and perfector of our faith." Why must we look to Jesus as the Source of endurance?

Stuart Briscoe writes, "The word perseverance isn't mentioned much nowadays because the concept is not very popular. Who wants to persevere? We'd rather trade it in. We'd rather act 'mature,' admit we made a mistake, and start again. Who wants to stick to something? We'd prefer to be happy with our immediate circumstances, but if we're not, then we can always change our circumstances.

In opposition to this, the Bible teaches that people who are truly the Lord's endure. . . . Theologians tell us that the reason we can persevere in the Lord is simply because the Lord is committed to persevering with us."[5]

DAY 3

Read James 1:2-4,12.

20. Verse 4—According to this verse, what does endurance produce in the believer?

21. Verses 2-3—According to these verses, what does God use as tools to produce endurance in the believer?

22. "Consider it all joy." What do you think is the relationship between joy and endurance?

"If your troubles, be they great or small, do not do you good they do you harm. There is such a thing as being made obstinate, hard, more clinging to earth than before by reason of griefs. And there is such a thing as a sorrow rightly borne being the very strength of a life, and delivering it from many a sin. There is nothing to be won in the perfecting of Christian character without our setting ourselves to it persistently, doggedly, continuously all through our lives. Brethren, be sure of this, you will never grow like Christ by mere wishing, by mere emotion, but only by continual faith, rigid self-control, and by continual struggle."[6] —Alexander Maclaren

23. What is attractive to you in other people about a spirit of joy in the midst of trials?

24. What do you think is the difference between living or existing through a trial and enduring through a trial?

25. From memory, write the verse you memorized on "temptation."

Remember that temptation can attack the believer in the area of endurance. Never be defeated with thoughts such as, "I don't know that endurance is such a great attribute, if it means that I will have to suffer through various problems. There are worse things than mediocrity." These kinds of thoughts come from Satan, not from a loving God.

26. Yet, what is the alternative to mediocrity? (Refer to question 20.)

27. Is this worth suffering? Explain.

"It is entirely possible to be in the will of God and still endure difficulties. Throughout our Christian lives, God will use difficult situations as a way of developing our characters, and we can never become mature Christians without them. There is no armchair correspondence course for becoming a mature Christian—we must all go through struggles to get there. So, we must learn to embrace difficulties and trials as opportunities for developing spiritual muscle. We need these times and should not shy away from them. Don't pray for an easy life. Pray for the strength to become a steadfast Christian."[7] —Floyd McClung

28. What is a trial that you are facing right now? It could be an illness of someone you love, or it could be a class at school you are struggling with.

Why can you choose to be thankful for this? (Refer to questions 20 and 26.)

29. James 1:12—According to this verse, how is endurance specifically rewarded?

DAY 4

Read Romans 15:4-6.

30. From memory, write the verse you memorized on "a love for God's Word."

31. Romans 15:4—How do you think the Bible encourages us to endure or continue in our Christian walk today?

32. Based on your own experience, why is endurance so important for a serious study of the Bible?

33. How is endurance profitable if you are to continue this discipleship course?

34. Verse 5—According to this verse, what is the source of our endurance (perseverance)?

35. Verses 5-6—For what purpose is endurance given?

36. How do you think relationships between people benefit from endurance and patience?

37. From what you have discovered about the Lord in your own life, how is He an Example of endurance, of long-suffering in relationships?

38. What example does He set for you?

"God sticks to His relationship. He establishes a personal relationship with us and stays with it. The central reality for Christians is the personal, inalterable, persevering commitment that God makes to us. Perseverance is not the result of our determination, it is the result of God's faithfulness. We survive in the way of faith not because we have extraordinary stamina but because God is righteous. Christian discipleship is a process of paying more and more attention to God's righteousness and less and less attention to our own; finding the meaning of our lives not by probing our moods and motives and morals but by believing in God's will and purposes; making a map of the faithfulness of God, not charting the rise and fall of our enthusiasms. It is out of such a reality that we acquire perseverance."[8] —Jim Peterson

DAY 5

Yesterday's study taught us about endurance in regard to Bible study and relationships. Today we will look at a passage that teaches us about perseverance in prayer.

39. As hard as it is to admit, sometimes, we are all dependent on others. Rare are the days when we need assistance from no one. Below you will read a variety of examples of requests that people ask of others. Write down typical responses when you ask. . .

  • a sales clerk to help you find a particular item.

  • a stranger for directions in how to find your destination.

  • a teacher for help with a problem you do not understand.

  • a friend for advice.

40. Describe possible motives that would cause these people to respond in the manner you just wrote.

Read Luke 11:5-13.

41. **Verses 5-8—When friendship was not enough, what finally got the man out of bed?**

42. **If a friend finds it within himself to respond to the persistent request of another friend, how must God respond to the persistent requests of His children. (Also compare with question 40.)**

43. **Verses 11-12—What is the response of a typical father to requests made by his children?**

44. **Verse 13—Yet, how does the Fatherhood of God extend beyond a typical Father?**

45. **Verses 9-10—What do these verses teach you about endurance in prayer?**

46. **How does this passage encourage you when you do not immediately receive the requests for which you ask?**

"O what a deep heavenly mystery this is of persevering prayer. The God who has promised, who longs, whose fixed purpose it is to give the blessing, holds it back. It is to Him a matter of such deep importance that His friends on earth should know and fully trust their rich Friend in heaven, that He trains them, in the school of answer delayed, to find out how their perseverance really does prevail, and what the mighty power is they can wield in heaven, if they do but set themselves to it."[9] —Andrew Murray

[1] Max Lucado, *No Wonder They Call Him the Savior* (Portland, Oregon: Multnomah, 1986), 60. Used by permission.
[2] Permission to quote the poem by Amy Carmichael is gratefully acknowledged and is used by permission of Christian Literature Crusade, Fort Washington, PA.
[3] Michael Griffiths, *The Example of Jesus* (reproduced by permission of William Neill-Hall Ltd., Cornwall, England), 90.
[4] John W. Sanderson, *The Fruit of the Spirit* (Phillipsburg, New Jersey: Presbyterian and Reformed Publishing Company, 1984, 1985), 90-91. Used by permission.
[5] Stuart Briscoe, *How to Be a Motivated Christian* (Wheaton, Illinois: Victor Books, 1987), 142-143.
[6] Alexander Maclaren, *Exposition of Holy Scripture, Hebrews-1 John* (Grand Rapids, Michigan: Baker Book House, 1974, 1977), 359.
[7] Taken from *Basic Discipleship* by Floyd McClung. © 1988, 1990 by Floyd McClung. Used with permission from InterVarsity Press, P.O. Box 1400, Downers Grove, IL 60515.
[8] Jim Peterson, *A Long Obedience in the Same Direction* (Downers Grove, Illinois: InterVarsity Press, 1980), 128-129.
[9] Andrew Murray, *With Christ in the School of Prayer* (Virginia Beach, Virginia: CBN University Press, 1978), 64-65.

WEEK 12
REEDEEMING THE TIME

DAY 1

In a study on becoming Christlike, we must take the opportunity to emphasize the use of time. As Anne Ortlund writes,

"How you spend your time reveals your life; it uncovers your desires, your goals, your weaknesses, your heart—the real you."[1]

Even though some things are pressing and urgent, they are not necessarily the most important. We convince ourselves that we will become more Christlike—more Christ-focused—later. When I am older I will devote more time to God. When my schedule lightens up I will obey Him. When I am out of high school I will have more time. Do not be deceived. You are becoming today what you will be tomorrow. And for some of us, tomorrow never comes.

"The character and career of a young person are determined largely by how and with whom he spends his spare time. He cannot regulate school or office hours—those are determined for him—but he can say what he will do before and after. . .Habits are formed in youth that make or mar a life. Leisure hours constitute a glorious opportunity or a subtle danger. Each moment of the day is a gift from God and should be husbanded with miserly care, for time is life measured out to us for work."[2] —J. Oswald Sanders

Read Psalm 31:14-15.

1. Verse 15—We try to make time tangible with our watches, calendars, and other time pieces, but who literally has a grasp on time?

2. Verse 15—According to this verse, where does this place every moment of your life?

3. Verse 14—Did this truth leave the psalmist secure or anxious?

4. What was Jesus' perspective of the time allotted to Him?

John 7:6

John 17:1

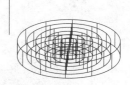

> "Time is a creature—a created thing—and a gift. We cannot make any more of it. We can only receive it and be faithful stewards in the use of it."[3]
> —Elisabeth Elliot

"Then David said to Gad, 'I am in great distress. Let us now fall into the hand of the Lord for His mercies are great, but do not let me fall into the hand of man'" (2 Sam. 24:14).

5. Is there any other hand with which you would entrust the boundaries of your life? A parent? Medical science? Yourself? Why or why not?

Read Acts 17:26-28.

6. How do these verses relate God with the time span allotted to you for your life?

7. Verse 27—What is the ultimate purpose of all time given to man on earth?

DAY 2

Read Psalm 90:12.

8. While the week, the month, the year, and the decade are all significant for calculating time, with what measurement will the wise person see time?

How do you think the years, decades and centuries will be affected as time is viewed in this way?

> "Time can be lost, but it can never be retrieved. It cannot be hoarded; it must be spent. Nor can it be postponed. If it is not used productively, it is irretrievably lost."[5]
> —J. Oswald Sanders

"The most difficult discovery I've been forced to learn about the abundant life is to live one day at a time and receive fresh grace from the Lord for each day. God has graciously measured out life. . .so that we can be present in the present with the power of his presence."[4] —Lloyd John Ogilvie

Read Psalm 39:4-5.

9. In verse 4, what does the psalmist pray for?

10. And what does the Lord reveal to him in verse 5?

11. Why do you think we most often lack this perspective?

12. How do you think our lives would be affected if we reflected on and lived by this truth?

Read Psalm 89:48.

13. What inevitably comes to all with the passage of time?

14. If death came knocking on your door today, would you have any regrets? If yes, what?

15. You only have one life. Why is it important that you not look back on it with regret?

16. How can you begin now to live a life without regret?

"Time is the one resource which we cannot manufacture. It is a non-renewable resource which limits our ability to experience all that we can. In a culture as wealthy as ours, there is no scarcity of money; but every day we feel the frustration of not having enough time to do all the things we desire."[6]
—George Barna

DAY 3

Read Ephesians 5:15-17.

"Therefore be careful how you walk. . ."

17. Imagine that everyone had to walk to school on a tightrope that was 150 feet above the ground. What would be the significance of every step?

18. Similarly, how is each moment significant in your Christian walk?

19. What might be some unwise moves on a tightrope 150 feet above the ground?

"Do not turn to the right nor to the left; turn your foot from evil"
(Prov. 4:27).

20. Why are Proverbs 4:27 and Ephesians 5:15-16 such wise counsel for the Christian who is determined to remain on the straight and narrow?

21. "Because the days are evil." Paul doesn't say to make the most of your time because "time is money" or because "you only go around

> "There will be time, depend upon it, for everything God wants us to do."
> —Elisabeth Elliot

once," but because the days are evil. What do you think is the warning here?

22. Ephesians 5:17—According to this verse, what is a wise use of your time?

"Teach me to do Thy will, for Thou art my God; let Thy good Spirit lead me on level ground" (Ps. 143:10).

23. According to the following verses, what is the Lord's will for our lives?

Joshua 1:8

Micah 6:8

Romans 12:2

1 Thessalonians 5:17

Hebrews 10:25

24. As these things become priorities in your use of time, how might the rest of your schedule be affected?

"In my creature impatience I am often caused to wish that there were some way to bring modern Christians into a deeper spiritual life painlessly by short easy lessons; but such wishes are vain. No short cut exists. God has not bowed to our nervous haste nor embraced the methods of our machine age. It is well that we accept the hard truth now: The man who would know God must give time to Him. He must count no time wasted which is spent in the cultivation of His acquaintance. He must give himself to meditation and prayer hours on end."[8] —A. W. Tozer

DAY 4

Read 2 Peter 3:8-18.

25. Verse 8—What is the Lord's perspective of time?

26. How do the following verses describe the finality of time?

verse 10

verse 12

27. **Verse 9—Why has this been delayed?**

28. **Verse 13–Yet how does the end of time actually mark a new beginning?**

29. **From memory, write the verse you memorized on "motives."**

30. **According to the following verses, the certainty of such events as described in today's passage should motivate us to do what with the time we have left?**

    verse 11

    verse 14

    verse 18

> "Time is a precious commodity. I refuse to allow what little time I have to be contaminated by self-pity, anxiety, or boredom. . .I will drink each minute as though it is my last. When tomorrow comes, today will be gone forever. While it is here, I will use it for loving and giving. Today I will make a difference."[10]
> —Max Lucado

> "After making a generous allowance of eight hours a day for sleep and rest—a few really need more than that—three hours a day for meals and social interaction, ten hours a day for work and travel on five days, there still remain no fewer than thirty-five hours unaccounted for in each week. What happens to them? How are the extra two days in the week invested? The whole of man's contribution to the kingdom of God might well turn upon how those crucial hours are employed. They will determine whether his life will be commonplace or extraordinary."[9] —J. Oswald Sanders

31. **Verses 16-17—If we do not make wise use of our time, how does it leave us vulnerable?**

32. **How has today's study helped your view of today, this hour, this moment?**

DAY 5

As we wrap up this week's study, we will learn time management from one of the most unlikely of teachers. We will also discover what greatly hinders our redeeming the time—laziness.

Read Proverbs 6:6-11.

33. **When you come upon an ant hill, what kind of activity do you expect to see happening around it?**

"Go to the ant, O sluggard, observe her ways and be wise" (Prov. 6:6).

34. How is the wisdom of the ant described in verses 7-8?

35. We are more blessed than the ants with things like greater intelligence, ability, strength, and creativity. Yet what do you think are some things that we can learn from them?

"Poor is he who works with a negligent hand, but the hand of the diligent makes rich. He who gathers in summer is a son who acts wisely. But he who sleeps in harvest is a son who acts shamefully" (Prov. 10:4-5).

36. According to Proverbs 6:11 and the above verse, what are consequences for the sin of laziness?

"How long will you lie down, O sluggard?" (Prov. 6:9).

37. Laziness does not only expose itself in the literal position of "lying down." Sometimes it causes us to recline in other areas. Complete the sentences below based on the corresponding verses.

A. While the lazy person procrastinates doing the will of God, the diligent person. . . (Rom. 12:11).

B. While the lazy person is busy taking advantage of others, the diligent person. . . (Eph. 4:28).

C. While the lazy person's prayer life is hit and miss, the diligent person. . . (Jas. 5:16).

D. While the lazy person's relationships are weak and shallow, the diligent person . . . (1 Pet. 4:8).

38. Indicate how you spend your time in regard to the following activities. Use the words "tool" (you are diligent in this area) or "couch" (you are lazy in this area).

A. Daily devotional time with God _____

B. Homework _____

C. School _____

D. Tidiness _____

E. Serving others _____

F. Church participation _____

G. Job _____

H. Keeping physically in shape _____

39. From memory, write the verse you memorized on "wholeheartedness."

40. Look again at question 38 and write how God is specifically leading you to redeem the time.

[1] *Discipling One Another*, Anne Ortlund, 1983, Word Publishing, Nashville, Tennessee. All rights reserved.

[2] Taken from: *Spiritual Leadership* by J. Oswald Sanders. Copyright 1967, Moody Bible Institute of Chicago. Moody Press. Used by permission.

[3] Elisabeth Elliot, *Discipline, The Glad Surrender* (Old Tappan, New Jersey: Fleming H. Revell Company, 1982), 97.

[4] Lloyd John Ogilvie, *Lord of the Impossible* (Nashville: Abingdon Press, 1984), 75-76. Used by permission.

[5] J. Oswald Sanders, *Spiritual Leadership*.

[6] George Barna, *The Frog in the Kettle* (Ventura, California: Regal Books, 1990), 39.

[7] Elisabeth Elliot, *Discipline, The Glad Surrender*, 97.

[8] A. W. Tozer, *The Divine Conquest* (Urichsville, Ohio: Barbour and Company, 1950), 22.

[9] J. Oswald Sanders, *Spiritual Leadership*.

[10] From *On the Anvil* by Max Lucado © 1985. Used by permission of Tyndale House Publishers, Inc. All rights reserved.

Who is the 'self' in your self-control?

WEEK 13
SELF-CONTROL

SCRIPTURE MEMORY
Self-control
■ Proverbs 16:22
■ Proverbs 17:27
■ 1 Corinthians 9:26-27

DAY 1

In the Bible, self-control relates to a person's command over his own desires, passions, and appetites. It appears in the list which makes up the fruit of the Spirit.

1. Galatians 5:22-23—After you read through this passage, write the fruit of the Spirit mentioned in these verses.

2. 2 Peter 1:5-7—Peter also includes self-control in his list of Christian virtues. Read these verses and write the virtues listed in this passage.

Self-control is probably most appreciated when we are confronted with a person who lacks it. We may not be able to pinpoint the characteristics of self-control, but we can easily describe a person who needs to get control of himself. But as you think about the attributes you listed for questions 1 and 2, you will realize that self-control is one of the most sought-after qualities of Christians today. Most important, the Bible teaches that self-control is one characteristic that will always be present where the Spirit is present. In other words, self-control must be present in the life of the believer.

On the other hand, "self" actually is not the source of self-control. Water will not flow from an empty well. If we feel we are lacking self-control, we will not be able to "drum up" a reserve supply from within ourselves.

"Consistent victory in my life is never the result of my trying to become more self-controlled. Think about it. How can self be more self-controlled? Can a wild animal tame itself? Would a puppy ever give itself a bath? Of course not. These things run contrary to natural instinct. In the same way self is never going to deprive self of something desirable.
Victory comes when I focus not on becoming more self-controlled but on the things of the Spirit. It is then, and only then, that self-control and faithfulness are produced in my life. It is then that I experience the power necessary to overcome temptation."[1] —Charles Stanley

Read 2 Corinthians 3:5-6.

3. What does this reveal about the self?

4. What does this say about God?

"Self-control for God's person does not imply that with severe self-discipline I can control my conduct. . .Self-control for the Christian means that my 'self,' my whole being, body, soul, spirit comes under the control of Christ. It means that I am an individual governed by God. . .It means giving up my rights. It goes beyond day-dreaming about being a delightful sort of soul. It gets down to the grass roots where I relinquish my self-rule and turn myself over irrevocably to God."[2] —W. Phillip Keller

5. From memory, write the verse you memorized on "who you are in Christ."

6. So who must be the "self" in our "self-control"? (Refer to questions 4 and 5.)

"'I am the vine, you are the branches; he who abides in Me, and I in him, he bears much fruit; for apart from Me you can do nothing'" (John 15:5).

DAY 2

Read Proverbs 25:28.

7. How does this proverb describe the person lacking self-control?

In ancient times a city without walls was a city without defense or identity. Without walls, the city would become vulnerable to foes on every side.
In this verse we find that, without self-control, our lives are like cities without walls. Eugene Peterson gives us a modern paraphrase of Proverbs 25:28:

"A person without self-control is like a house with its doors and windows knocked out."[4]

A house without windows or doors becomes an open invitation for intruders. When we lack self-control, our lives become an open invitation for another kind of intruder: the Enemy. He wastes no time in ransacking our lives and leaving behind his own odds and ends. Soon this becomes evident in our conduct and behavior.

8. Read Galatians 5:19-21. According to these verses, what are the evidences that a life has been ransacked by the Enemy?

9. How could a person use self-control as a dead-bolt lock in the face of the Enemy and the things you just listed?

"When we know Christ, we shall know ourselves; when He is the self of ourselves, then, and only then, shall we reverence and can we control the inner man."[3]
—Alexander Maclaren

"Do not give the devil an opportunity" (Eph. 4:27).

10. **How might a lack of self-control in just one of the areas listed in question 8 give the Enemy access to other areas?**

11. **Why do you think the flesh is helpless in overcoming the things you listed for question 8?**

"The need for continual vigilance and self-control comes from the very make of our souls, for our nature is not a democracy, but a kingdom. In us all there are passions, desires, affections, all of which may lead to vice or to virtue: and all of which evidently call out for direction, for cultivation, and often for repression."[5] —Alexander Maclaren

Read Proverbs 16:32.

12. **We might consider things like aggression, rage, physical prowess, and domination over others as strengths in a mighty warrior. Yet what does Proverbs 16:32 teach us about real strength?**

13. **While the world's value system encourages us to strengthen the outer person, God says that the center of real strength is the inner person. When the outer person gives in to sin, it is the inner person giving it permission to do so. With this in mind, why do you think self-control is so important to the inner person?**

14. **According to the first part of Proverbs 16:32, what is one evidence that a person possesses self-control?**

15. **"He who rules his spirit." Too often, we let our spirit or feelings or attitude rule us. We let them dictate our responses and our moods. But self-control means that we choose not to let these things control us. Maybe there are things in your life that you have allowed to control you. How might you benefit from self-control in the following areas? Complete these sentences:**

    A. Instead of depression, I choose. . .

    B. Instead of being irritated, I choose. . .

    C. Instead of worry, I choose. . .

    D. Instead of greed, I choose. . .

"A sound mind makes for a robust body,
but runaway emotions corrode the bones" (Prov. 14:30).

DAY 3

"Limits are good. They allow for godly interaction. Almost everything we live with is limited. Fire is good for cooking. It is not good if the flames leap above the stove and catch the ceiling on fire."[6] —Lois Mowday

16. What might result if we did not set limits in the following areas?

    A. Spending money

    B. Recreation

    C. Time watching TV

    D. Work

Read 1 Corinthians 9:24-27.

17. What types of limits or restrictions must a runner or any athlete set for himself or herself? Why?

18. From memory, write the verse you memorized on "endurance."

19. Verses 24-25—According to Paul, why do athletes exercise self-control and endurance in their physical training?

"We exercise control over ourselves when we have some clear ambition or aim. Left to ourselves we will always choose actual evil or lesser good as our goal."[7] —John W. Sanderson

20. Verse 27—The runner's opponents are other runners; but in the Christian race, where does Paul indicate that he finds his greatest opposition? Why?

21. "Make it my slave." When do you think this opponent (question 20) becomes the believer's slave?

22. How is this possible? (Refer to question 4.)

23. What could happen if you drove away in a car without any pre-determined destination?

24. Verse 26—When do Christians give the appearance of running without aim or beating the air in the Christian race?

25. Verses 25b and 27b—What must we remember when we are tempted to quit the race?

Imagine the thrill of the Olympian when the official places the gold medal around his or her neck. Yet it pales in comparison to the forthcoming day when the wreath imperishable is positioned on your head by hands that bear the scars of nails.

DAY 4

26. Proverbs 14:17, 29—How are the actions of the one who is quick tempered contrasted with the actions of the one who is slow to anger?

27. Proverbs 19:19—Notice how a man of anger is described in this verse. What similarities do you see in the behavior of people suffering from substance addictions today?

28. Do you think that all sin can become addictive? Explain.

29. From memory, write the verse you memorized on "hating sin."

30. In what situations are you easily angered?

"You tell yourself in words, images, and attitudes the very things that cause you to feel anger. 'Isn't it terrible how Jim always keeps me waiting?' 'It's disgusting and rotten that I'm the one who gets stuck with the job of mowing the lawn and raking the leaves while she sits inside drinking coffee!' 'It makes me sick the way their dog eats better than a lot of people in the world.' The truth is, such things are not horrendous at all. It is unpleasant when things don't go as you'd like them to do or when someone says unkind words to you, but it's not awful or terrible."[8] —William Backus and Marie Chapian

31. How is anger a choice?

32. Proverbs 22:24-25—If you place yourself around a person who is inclined to fits of temper, how will it impact your proneness toward anger?

33. Read the following verses. Rather than allowing anger to rub off on you, what can you do in the face of anger? And what effect can these responses have on the one who is angry?

	Action	Result
A. Proverbs 15:1		
B. Proverbs 25:15		
C. Ecclesiastes 10:4		

Read James 1:19-20.

34. **Verse 20—Why is it so important that we exercise self-control in regard to our temper?**

35. **Verse 19—When do our ears and mouths become the tools of self-control?**

"Do not be overcome by evil, but overcome evil with good"
(Rom. 12:21).

36. **Proverbs 17:27-28—How else does the mouth benefit from self-control?**

37. **From memory, write the verse you memorized on "time."**

38. **How could your time management benefit from self-control?**

39. **Proverbs 25:16—Gluttony is a subtle sin. How can our eating habits benefit from self-control?**

Our desire for food is not the only appetite that needs to surrender to self-control. Tomorrow we will look at the lust of the flesh in regard to sexual temptation and the tragedies that come to those who give in to it.

DAY 5

Read Genesis 34:1-31.

40. **Verse 1—Who is Dinah?**

41. Verse 2—Who is Shechem?

42. Verse 2—How did Shechem lose control?

43. Verse 7—What was the initial response of Jacob's sons to what happened?

44. Verses 8-10—What does Hamor propose as an agreement?

45. Verses 11-12—What does Shechem vow of himself?

46. Verses 14-17—Yet, how do Jacob's sons respond?

47. Verse 13—What was really behind their negotiations?

48. How did Hamor and Shechem respond?

   verse 18

   verse 19

   verses 20-24

49. Verses 25-29—What did Jacob's sons do?

50. Verses 7 and 31—What motivated such actions?

51. What does this incident teach you about the importance of self-control?

52. How do the following verses describe Shechem's affection for Dinah?

   verse 3

   verse 8

   verse 19

"Love does not act unbecomingly; it does not seek its own"
(1 Cor. 13:5).

53. Shechem seemed to have been at the mercy of his passions. He was overcome with "love." But how is real love contrasted with Shechem's actions, especially as you consider the above verse?

54. How will real love express self-control even when two people are in love?

[1] Charles Stanley, *The Wonderful Spirit Filled Life* (Nashville: Thomas Nelson, 1992), 120-121.

[2] W. Phillip Keller, *A Gardener Looks at the Fruits of the Spirit* (Waco, Texas: Word Books, 1979), 177, 181.

[3] Alexander Maclaren, *Exposition of Holy Scripture, Proverbs* (Grand Rapids, Michigan: Baker Book House 1974, 1977), 277.

[4] Eugene H. Peterson, *The Message* (Colorado Springs: NavPress, 1993, 1994, 1995).

[5] Alexander Maclaren, *Exposition of Holy Scripture, Proverbs*, 275.

[6] Lois Mowday, *The Source* (Colorado Springs: NavPress, 1988), 230.

[7] John W. Sanderson, *The Fruit of the Spirit* (Phillipsburg, New Jersey: Presbyterian and Reformed Publishing Company, 1984, 1985), 138. Used by permission.

[8] William Backus/Marie Chapian, *Telling Yourself the Truth* (Minneapolis: Bethany House Publishers, 1980), 53-54.

[9] Jerry Bridges, *The Practice of Godliness* (Colorado Springs: NavPress, 1983), 172.

WEEK 14
SEXUAL MORALITY

DAY 1

1. From memory, write the verse you memorized on "humility."

In many ways, our generation has chosen to live under an umbrella of self-gratification—the immediate, the immodest, and the immoral. The human sex drive is in high gear, and the flesh has taken over the driver's seat. If we are not careful, we soon find ourselves in the back seat, far away from the brakes, staring out the window, and watching the messages of the billboards telling us we can do little more than give in. And many do.

But Christianity provides us with a new Driver and a new license as well—a license to say, "No."

"For you were called to freedom, brethren; only do not turn your freedom into an opportunity for the flesh, but through love serve one another" (Gal. 5:13).

Sexual sin never involves only one person, and it rarely affects only two. That's why humility becomes so important as we consider the topic of sexual morality. Humility looks out for the interests of others. As we have studied, a person of humility regards others as more important than himself or herself. Likewise, our value system in regard to sexuality will largely depend on how we value one another.

"Honor all men" (1 Pet. 2:17).

2. Romans 12:10—Where lies the commitment of devotion, brotherly love, and honor? Cirlcle one.

    A. with self   B. with Christ   C. with one another

3. What do you think it means to honor another person?

4. How can this impact your relationships with your family and friends?

"There is an appointed time for everything. And there is a time for every event under heaven . . . a time to embrace, and a time to shun embracing" (Eccl. 3:1,5).

Think through the following:

- Does it honor a person when you break up with him or her and date someone else two days later?
- Does it honor your future mate when you carelessly give your kisses away?
- Does it honor someone when the locker room becomes your audience regarding last night's date?
- Does it honor a brother or sister in Christ when you allow someone else to verbally degrade him or her without you, in kindness, saying something to show where you stand on relationships?
- Does it honor the other person, that person's future mate, or that person's future children when you have sex with him or her outside of marriage?

Imagine the opportunity we would have to give the world a picture of what Jesus is like if we would esteem each other with honor in our dating lives!

5. From memory, write the verse you memorized on "thought life."

6. How does your thought life impact the way you honor your brothers and sisters in Christ?

7. How does your thought life impact your value system regarding sexual morality?

DAY 2

"For this cause a man shall leave his father and his mother, and shall cleave to his wife; and they shall become one flesh" (Gen. 2:24).

Read Hebrews 13:4.

8. "Let marriage be held in honor among all." How do you think our society, as a whole, has fallen short of this ideal?

Considering what you just wrote, why can you be grateful that the institute of marriage originated in the heart of God, and was not the brainchild of human beings?

"Let the marriage bed be undefiled."

9. How does one who is married bring defilement to his or her marriage bed?

10. How do you think the sexual experiments of adolescence could defile one's marriage bed later on?

11. Read Hebrews 13:4 again. When someone is contemplating, "How far should I go?" what should he or she consider?

12. Imagine that today your future spouse is formulating some sexual guidelines for his or her dating life. This person has you, though nameless and faceless, on his or her heart preparing these standards. What are some principles that he or she could come up with that would not bring defilement to your marriage bed? In other words, what do you hope is on his or her list?

13. Most often we think of finding the right person. But why is it more important that we focus on becoming the right person?

Elisabeth Elliot writes, "From a respectful distance, with no knowledge on his part, I had the opportunity to observe the character of Jim Elliot. . .I watched him in the dining-hall lines. . .a man who was careful with his time. I watched his friendliness and enthusiasm. I knew what kind of student he was. I watched him wrestle (he won a championship in four states), watched him lead the Foreign Missions Fellowship, heard him pray. There was nothing pompous or stuffy about him. I noticed his clothes. He spent very little on them—wore the same two or three pairs of trousers and the same jacket and sweater for years. He had hardly any notion of styles or colors, but he was not sloppy. Not that this proved he was the man I was looking for, but it gave me a hint that his primary concern was not clothes. When we began to get better acquainted through conversation, I found my hunches verified. Long before I had any reason to think he might be interested in me, I had put him down as the sort of man I hoped to marry. Kissing and holding hands would have added nothing to this conviction (anybody can kiss and hold hands). On the contrary, in fact, it would have subtracted something very important. I wanted to marry a man prepared to swim against the tide.

I took it for granted that there must be a few men left in the world who had that kind of strength. I assumed that those men would also be looking for women of principle. I did not want to be among the marked-down goods on the bargain table, cheap because they'd been pawed over. Crowds collect there. It is only the few who will pay full price, 'You get what you pay for.' "[1]

14. What will be the summary of your sexual history if you are not prepared to swim against the tide? (Refer to question 8.)

DAY 3

We are surrounded by the mentality that suggests God's commandments were written in chalk rather than in stone. It insinuates that God may have been a little less forthright in His laws had He only known then what medical science knows today. But knowledge is of little benefit to One who is omniscient (all-knowing). What could He learn? And what use would an eraser be to One who is infallible? He has nothing to add to His laws and nothing to take from them, because He is perfect and the Source of them.

We live in a day when the definitions of sin seem vague and obscure. This is especially true in regard to sexual morality. Today's passage will clear up the confusion as it gives specific names to immorality and lists them all under the category of sin.

Read 1 Corinthians 6:9-11.

15. Verse 9—What is true of those who are unrighteous or wicked?

16. Verses 9-10—According to these verses, what are the specific deeds of unrighteousness or wickedness?

"Do you not know that the unrighteous shall not inherit the kingdom of God? Do not be deceived. . ." (1 Cor. 6:9).

17. Fornication is a word in the Bible that refers to sexual sin outside of marriage, including premarital sex. What does the Bible say to emotional responses like, "It's OK to have sex if you really love the person," or "We plan to get married anyway"?

18. From memory, write the verse you memorized on "a love for God's Word."

19. Which of these two is unchanging?

  A. Emotions   B. God's Word

20. On what, then, must you base your standards for how far you should go sexually prior to marriage?

"And in the same way also the men abandoned the natural function of the woman and burned in their desire toward one another, men with men committing indecent acts and receiving in their own persons the due penalty of their error" (Rom. 1:27).

21. When you consider today's passage (1 Cor. 6:9-11) and the above verse, why does homosexuality fall under the category of sin?

We will go to great lengths to justify our sin. Today homosexuality is not regarded as a perversion in the eye of society, but as an issue of genetics. While the Bible clearly classifies homosexuality as a perverse act, it does support the case of heredity. That's right. We were all born with the capacity for homosexuality and every other sin known to mankind! It is in our heritage. Sin is manifested in different ways, but it will manifest itself in every person. That doesn't mean we should resign ourselves to sin's control. Some people are more prone to alcoholism (drunkenness is mentioned in today's passage), but does that mean we should condone it? According to the Bible, homosexuality, like other sins, is an issue of the will. It is a choice.

22. Verse 11—Rather than justifying our sins of fornication, homosexuality, and drunkenness, how have we been set free from them?

"'Come now, and let us reason together,' says the Lord, 'Though your sins are as scarlet, they will be as white as snow; Though they are red like crimson, they will be like wool'" (Isa. 1:18).

23. How does the above verse minister to you in regard to past failures in the area of sexual sin?

24. From memory, write the verse you memorized on "holiness."

25. How does this verse relate to your sex life?

It is naive to think that you can experiment with sex during your teen years and lock the door of your memory when you are married. God forgives, forgets, and restores. Sexual immorality is not the unpardonable sin! But don't be deceived; the consequences and effects of sexual sin are different from other sins as we shall discover in tomorrow's passage.

DAY 4

Read 1 Corinthians 6:13-20.

26. Verse 13—The need for food and the hunger for it is natural for the body. But over-indulgence is a sin. Even so, how does Paul make a difference between the parts of the body and the body as a whole? What does he say about the body?

27. In what other ways is your body unique according to the following verses?

verse 13

verse 15

verse 19

28. Verses 15-16, 18—According to these verses, what degrades the body?

29. Verse 15—Who else is degraded when believers participate in sexual immorality?

30. Verse 18—Why does Paul single out sexual sin with such a strong warning?

"That is why I say to run from sex sin. No other sin affects the body as this one does. When you sin this sin it is against your own body" (1 Cor. 6:18).⁴

"Beloved, I urge you as aliens and strangers to abstain from fleshly lusts, which wage war against the soul" (1 Pet. 2:11).

31. From memory, write the verse you memorized on "self-control."

32. The world is sending out mixed signals. On one hand it encourages you to be all that you can be. After all, you can do anything you set your mind to do. On the other hand, it also tells you that you can only do what your body dictates that you do—that the ideals of waiting for sexual intimacy until you are married are unrealistic; that you are, at best, a slave of your own flesh. How does God's fruit of self-control contradict such notions?

33. The picture of oneness sanctioned by God for two people in a marriage relationship is really a picture of something even more divine. According to verses 15-17, what is this?

"There's more to sex than mere skin on skin. Sex is as much spiritual mystery as physical fact. As written in Scripture, 'The two become one.' Since we want to become spiritually one with the Master, we must not pursue the kind of sex that avoids commitment and intimacy, leaving us more lonely than ever, the kind of sex that can never become one." (1 Cor. 6:16-17).[5]

"The Christian idea of marriage is based on Christ's words that a man and wife are to be regarded as a singe organism—for that is what the words 'one flesh' would be in modern English. And the Christians believe that when He said this He was not expressing a sentiment but stating a fact—just as one is stating a fact when one says that a lock and its key are one mechanism, or that a violin and a bow are one musical instrument. The inventor of the human machine was telling us that its two halves, the male and the female, were made to be combined together in pairs, not simply on the sexual level, but totally combined. The monstrosity of sexual intercourse outside marriage is that those who indulge in it are trying to isolate one kind of union (the sexual) from all other kinds of union which were intended to go along with it and make up the total union. The Christian attitude does not mean that there is anything wrong in sexual pleasure, any more than about the pleasure of eating. It means that you must not isolate that pleasure and try to get it by itself, any more than you ought to try to get the pleasures of taste without swallowing and digesting, by chewing things and spitting them out again."[6]
—C. S. Lewis

34. What can the longing for intimacy with other human beings teach us about the real longing of the human heart?

"'But cleave unto the Lord your God, as ye have done unto this day'" (Josh. 23:8).[7]

35. 1 Corinthians 6:20—What commitment has God made to you and your body?

What is the only genuine option left for your response? Why?

"Know that the Lord Himself is God; It is He who has made us, and not we ourselves; We are His people and the sheep of His pasture" (Ps. 100:3).

DAY 5

Read 1 Thessalonians 4:1-8.

36. From memory, write the verse you memorized on "endurance."

37. How does 1 Thessalonians 4:1 encourage you to endure in your Christian walk and your pursuit of Christlikeness?

38. How is Christlikeness specifically accomplished in. . .

. . .turning away from what is evil (verse 3)

. . .turning toward what is right (verse 4)

39. According to the following verses, what makes the principles of this passage, or any other passage, credible?

verse 2

verse 3

verse 7

verse 8

40. Why can you trust God with your dating life?

"For this is the will of God, your sanctification; that is, that each of you know how to possess his own vessel in sanctification and honor" (1 Thess. 4:3-4).

41. Based on the above verse, explain how you can benefit from the following.

- Deciding your limits before you date

- Selecting a couple of trustworthy friends with whom you could share these limits

- Communicating these limits to those you date

- Refusing to date those who do not share your convictions

- Accepting God's love and forgiveness over past failure

- Surrounding yourself with other believers who share the same standards

- Limiting your time alone together with someone of the opposite sex

42. As you now bring your dating life before God, make a list of standards that you believe would please Him regarding whom you will date and how you will behave physically. Be specific!

43. What is stopping you from embracing these standards as your own?

[1] Elisabeth Elliot, *Passion and Purity* (Grand Rapids, Michigan: Fleming H. Revell, 1984), 128-129.
[2] Lois Mowday, *The Snare* (Colorado Springs: NavPress, 1988), 231.
[3] Chap Clark, *The Next Time I Fall in Love* (El Cajon, California: Grow For It Books, 1987), 70.
[4] *The Living Bible*, (Wheaton, Illinois: Tyndale House Publishers, 1971, 1973).
[5] Eugene H. Peterson, *The Message* (Colorado Springs: NavPress, 1993, 1994, 1995).
[6] *Mere Christianity* by C. S. Lewis copyright © C. S. Lewis Pte. Ltd. 1942, 1943, 1944, 1952. Extract reprinted by permission.
[7] King James Version, *The Holy Bible* (New York: American Bible Society, 1974).

WEEK 15
DISCIPLINE

DAY 1

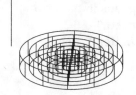

This week, think of discipline as a college course. The first semester will focus on the God-enforced discipline of correction. The second semester will concentrate on the self-enforced discipline of self-management. Both aspects of discipline make up a complete curriculum. Both are crucial for the one whose major is godliness.

1. What actions by your friends most commonly call for parental discipline?

2. Have you ever been inwardly glad when a friend was disciplined? Do you think this revealed a lack of genuine friendship, or was it the evidence of it? Explain.

Read Psalm 89:30-34.

3. Verses 30-31—What specific actions noted here invite the discipline of the Lord?

"If his children refuse to do what I tell them, if they refuse to walk in the way I show them, if they spit on the directions I give them and tear up the rules I post for them. . ."[1] *(Ps. 89:30-31).*

4. Recall a time in your life when your actions reflected the type of attitude described in these verses.

"I'll rub their faces in the dirt of their rebellion and make them face the music'"[2] *(Ps. 89:32).*

> "Some people seem to think that unless some external calamity befalls a man when he sins, he is not being punished for his sin. But the most terrible punishment does not come in the form of external calamity, but in the form of the internal collapse of his personal powers and capacities. The most awful calamity that comes to a man is what happens in the man himself."[3]
> —Walter T. Conner

5. Verse 32—What is the warning here?

6. Look again at what you wrote on question 4. What did God use to discipline you in this situation? In other words, what did He allow to happen to you to bring you to repentance?

"For My eyes are on all their ways; they are not hidden from My face, nor is their iniquity concealed from My eyes" (Jer. 16:17).

7. Perhaps disobedience and rebellion are constantly in your heart even now. According to Jeremiah 16:17, what is true about the sin you embrace today?

8. What will inevitably happen? (Refer to question 5.)

9. You can repent now or face the consequences. What is your choice? Write it here.

10. Psalm 89:33-34—When we stray from godliness, what is true about God?

11. Why can you be thankful for the discipline of the Lord?

DAY 2

Read Hebrews 12:5-13.

12. What do you observe in young children who have had little or no discipline from their parents?

13. When a parent places no restrictions on a child, would you consider it an act of love or neglect? Explain.

14. Verse 8—To what does the Bible compare this type of relationship noted above?

15. Verse 6—What does this verse teach us about God?

16. Verse 7—When a person is disciplined by God, what does it reveal about the person?

17. How do the following verses compare the discipline of earthly fathers with the discipline of our heavenly Father?

    verse 9

    verse 10

18. Verses 5 and 9—How are we to respond to the discipline of the Lord?

19. From memory, write the verse you memorized on "holiness."

20. According to the following verses, what does the discipline of the Lord produce in us?

    verse 10

    verse 11

"God's goal in discipline is not simply to make us behave. His purpose is to make us holy, to bring us into conformity with His Son. He wants to build into our experience a hatred for sin similar to His own—a hatred that will cause us to separate ourselves not only from the practice of evil, but from the very appearance of it as well. Through this process, our character will be fine-tuned to reflect the character of Christ Himself. Because God knows us inside and out, He can tailor our discipline in such a way to accomplish just that."[4]
—Charles Stanley

21. Verses 12-13—So far, today's lesson has focused on the discipline of the Lord and how His firm hand strengthens our character. But we conclude with two verses that relate more to self-discipline. How might verses 12 and 13 instruct us in regard to strengthening our own character?

DAY 3

Read Deuteronomy 8:1-10.

22. Verse 1—What was God's plan for His people?

23. Verses 7-10—What were the specific benefits of His plan?

24. What did the people need to understand and apply before they would receive this promise?

    verse 1a

verse 3b

verse 6

25. The people had to learn that the Lord Himself was their trust and not His blessings. What did the Lord do to teach them this lesson? (verse 5)

26. Verses 2-3—How did He specifically discipline them?

27. With what, apart from Christ, do we sometimes try to satisfy our spiritual hunger, our innermost desires?

"Jesus therefore said to them, 'Truly, truly, I say to you, it is not Moses who has given you the bread out of heaven, but it is My Father who gives you the true bread out of heaven. . .I am the bread of life; he who comes to Me shall not hunger, and he who believes in Me shall never thirst'" (John 6:32, 35).

28. How has God abundantly provided for our spiritual needs?

29. Why do you think it often takes drastic discipline (question 26) from the Father before we will understand this?

30. How might self-discipline in the right areas (verse 6) cause the discipline of God to become unnecessary?

31. Think about a modern-day wilderness (verses 2-3) for you personally. For example: a lack of direction, a lack of purpose, deep unfulfilled longings. Then complete the sentence, My life feels like a modern-day wilderness when. . .

32. Describe a modern-day promised land (verses 7-10) for you personally. For example: a sense of success, a sense of fulfillment, a sense of security. Then complete the sentence, My life feels like a modern-day promised land when. . .

33. How do each of the above scenarios tempt us to become undisciplined in the things of God?

Modern-day wilderness

34. Circle the one which best describes where you are right now. How can you remain disciplined in the things of God as you experience it?

DAY 4

As we have studied this week, the discipline of our Father is crucial if we are to become godly men and women. Today we will look at how self-discipline trains us to become Christlike.

35. Describe the absurdity of a physical fitness plan that requires no self-discipline in regard to exercise or eating habits.

Read 1 Timothy 4:6-10.

Below you will find a variety of translations and paraphrases of 1 Timothy 4:7b.

"Discipline yourself for the purpose of godliness"
"Train yourself to be godly"
"Spend your time and energy in the exercise of keeping spiritually fit"
"Take time and trouble to keep yourself spiritually fit"
"Exercise daily in God, no spiritual flabbiness, please!"

36. What words above relate to self-discipline?

Look at the words you just wrote. How do they help you understand what it means to discipline yourself?

37. From memory, write the verse you memorized on "a love for God's Word."

38. According to the last half of verse 6, what are the tools of discipline that help train us in godliness?

39. How do you think self-discipline is beneficial in our reading, memorizing, and studying of the Bible?

40. How can you specifically apply the principles of verse 6 to your own life?

41. Why do you think we must remember that discipline is a tool used to produce godliness and not the essence of godliness itself?

"God doesn't love me more when I'm faithful in my prayer life. Reading the Bible every day doesn't earn me brownie points with God. We can't have the attitude that, 'I witnessed to somebody today, Lord, so now you've got to help me get that promotion I was hoping for.' That's legalism, trying to buy God's favor through good works, and it can't be done. . .Reading the Bible, praying, etc. won't buy us any special privileges with God, but they will help us function better and more efficiently in the spiritual realm, and in the long run, they help us become more like Jesus."[11] —Christopher B. Adsit

42. Verse 7—When must we use discipline as a shield over the ear?

43. From memory, write the verse you memorized on "motives."

44. When the circumstances are right, even a very lazy person can discipline himself or herself. It is amazing how the right "pay off" will propel us out of bed or activate us to complete even the most grueling tasks. What about you? All of the following rewards require a certain amount of discipline in a variety of areas. Rate each reward 1 through 5, with 5 being those which you are most willing to exercise self-discipline to possess.

_____The reward is a promotion	_____The reward is money
_____The reward is acceptance	_____The reward is a letter grade
_____The reward is recognition	_____The reward is better health
_____The reward is time with friends	_____The reward is a better appearance
_____The reward is knowledge	_____The reward is a sense of satisfaction

45. How does the first part of verse 8 describe the rewards of discipline like those above?

46. What reward is most worthy of self-discipline? Why?

47. Verse 10—Why is Jesus the Source of self-discipline and the work it produces?

DAY 5

"Not lagging behind in diligence, fervent in spirit, serving the Lord" (Rom. 12:11).

48. Why could the above verse be a description of the believer who is disciplined?

49. How do the following verses characterize the disciplined and undisciplined in regard to work?

	Disciplined	Undisciplined
Proverbs 10:4		
Proverbs 12:24		

50. What do the following verses also teach us about the rewards of discipline in regard to work?

Proverbs 17:2

Proverbs 22:29

"A lazy life is an empty life, but 'early to rise' gets the job done" (Prov. 12:27).[12]

"I fear our generation has come dangerously near the 'I'm-getting-tired-so-let's-just-quit' mentality. And not just in the spiritual realm. Dieting is a discipline, so we stay fat. Finishing school is a hassle, so we bail out. Cultivating a close relationship is painful, so we back off."[13] —Charles Swindoll

"The soul of the sluggard craves and gets nothing, but the soul of the diligent is made fat" (Prov. 13:4).

51. Proverbs 23:12—How is the disciplined or diligent soul made "fat"?

52. Proverbs 19:16—According to this verse, what becomes of the spiritual life of the disciplined and the spiritual life of the undisciplined?

53. 1 Thessalonians 5:17—What is the significance of discipline in regard to your prayer life, especially as you consider the command of this verse?

54. Galatians 6:1—How can the accountability of others help you have a disciplined walk with God?

"The totality of the believer's response is discipline. . .We might say that discipline is the disciple's 'career.' It defines the very shape of the disciple's life. . .Discipline is the believer's answer to God's call."[14]
—Elisabeth Elliot

"Let the righteous smite me in kindness and reprove me; it is oil upon the head; do not let my head refuse it" (Ps. 141:5).

"We're more familiar with behind-the-back criticism, airing each other's faults. We're more familiar with face-to-face blaming, the harsh and hostile pointing of the finger. We handle each other so roughly! We know plenty about each others' failures, but we know almost nothing about. . .humbly helping restore a brother from a fault of his, and so bearing each other's burdens."[15]
—Anne Ortlund

55. How does the knowledge that others will be meeting with you for discussion help you remain disciplined in completing your study of discipleship?

56. Why must our accountability ultimately be with God alone if we are to continue in a disciplined walk with Him for life?

"Unless the Lord builds the house, they labor in vain who build it; unless the Lord guards the city, the watchman keeps awake in vain" (Ps. 127:1).

[1] Eugene H. Peterson, *The Message* (Colorado Springs: NavPress, 1993, 1994, 1995).

[2] Ibid.

[3] Walter T. Conner, *The Gospel of Redemption* (Nashville: Broadman Press, 1945), 39.

[4] Charles Stanley, *How to Handle Adversity* (Nashville: Oliver-Nelson, a division of Thomas Nelson, Inc., 1989), 96.

[5] *The Student Bible, New International Version* (Grand Rapids, Michigan: Zondervan Bible Publishers, 1986).

[6] *The Living Bible* (Wheaton, Illinois: Tyndale House Publishers, 1971, 1973).

[7] J. B. Phillips, *The New Testament in Modern English* (New York: Macmillan Publishing Company, 1958, 1959, 1960, 1972).

[8] Eugene H. Peterson, *The Message*.

[9] Jerry Bridges, *The Practice of Godliness* (Colorado Springs: NavPress, 1983), 42.

[10] Reprinted from *The Pursuit of Holiness*. © 1978 by Jerry Bridges. Used by permission of NavPress, Colorado Springs, CO. All rights reserved.

[11] Christopher B. Adsit, *Personal Disciple-Making* (Nashville: Thomas Nelson Publishers, 1993), 199.

[12] Eugene H. Peterson, *The Message*.

[13] Taken from *Devotions for Growing Strong in the Seasons of Life*. Copyright © 1983 by Charles Swindoll, Inc. Used by permission of Zondervan Publishing House.

[14] Elisabeth Elliot, *Discipline, The Glad Surrender* (Old Tappan, New Jersey: Fleming H. Revell, 1982), 17.

[15] Anne Ortlund, *Discipling One Another* (Waco, Texas: Word Books, 1979, 1983), 141.

WEEK 16
TAMING THE TONGUE

Chuck Swindoll writes, "Without the tongue no mother could sing her baby to sleep tonight. No ambassador could adequately represent our nation. No teacher could stretch the minds of students. No officer could lead his fighting men in battle. No attorney could defend the truth in court. No pastor could comfort troubled souls. No complicated, controversial issue could ever be discussed and solved. Our entire world would be reduced to unintelligible grunts and shrugs. Seldom do we pause to realize just how valuable this strange muscle in our mouths really is. . .But the tongue is as volatile as it is vital."

SCRIPTURE MEMORY
The Tongue
■ Proverbs 18:21
■ Matthew 12:36-37
■ Ephesians 4:29

DAY 1

"If anyone thinks himself to be religious, and yet does not bridle his tongue, but deceives his own heart, this man's religion is worthless" (Jas. 1:26).

Read James 3:2-12.

1. **Verses 3-5—What do the horse's bit, the ship's rudder, and the human tongue share in common?**

2. **Verse 5—"So also the tongue is a small part of the body." Though the tongue is small in size, how do the following verses describe its massive influence?**

   verse 2

   verse 6

3. **Verses 7-8—How do the beasts, birds, reptiles, and creatures of the sea differ from the human tongue?**

4. **Verses 11-12—What is impossible in the natural world?**

5. **Verses 9-10—But when do we allow such contradictions to exist in us?**

6. Why are we only deceiving ourselves when we think it is OK to do so?

"Death and life are in the power of the tongue" (Prov. 18:21).

7. James 3:8 says that the tongue is "a restless evil and full of deadly poison." Poison is a means of bringing about death. Think about it. Our tongues have the power to destroy other people. What is another weapon of death that you think would make a good comparison to the tongue? Explain your comparison.

8. Undoubtedly, unkind remarks about other people hurt them. Flippant or careless words expressed in the heat of the moment can scar another for life. But how does what you say about another person affect you? (Refer to verse 6 and question 2.)

DAY 2

Yesterday we read how James compared the tongue to a fountain sending out both fresh and bitter water. Today's lesson begins with a passage giving specific examples of these.

Read Proverbs 15:1-4.

9. Identify the fresh and bitter water from each of the following verses.

	Fresh Water	Bitter Water
verse 1		
verse 2		
verse 4		

10. Verse 3—Why is this a sobering thought in regard to our speech?

"Even before there is a word on my tongue, behold, O Lord, Thou dost know all" (Ps. 139:4).

Read Psalm 52:1-4.

11. Describe the bitter water as indicated in the following verses.

verse 1a

verse 2

verse 3

verse 4

12. What does the comparison in verse 2 teach you about the tongue?

13. Verse 1—Of what would our tongues do well to boast?

"Help, Lord, for the godly man ceases to be, For the faithful disappear from among the sons of men" (Ps. 12:1).

14. According to Psalm 12:2-4, what did the psalmist state was the evidence that the people had lost the objective of a godly life?

15. Compare the bitter water from Psalm 12:2-4 with the fresh water in Psalm 12:6.

16. Identify the fresh and bitter water from the following verses.

Ephesians 4:25

Ephesians 5:3-4

"Caustic comments may be socially acceptable, but they have no place in the kingdom of God. Sarcasm is a thinly veiled attempt to impress people by highlighting the faults of others. Its humor is always at the expense of another person. Using sarcasm sometimes reveals that we have been hurt or offended by others and have not had the courage to deal with it openly. Instead, we allow bitterness to grow in our hearts."[3] —Floyd McClung

17. Ephesians 4:29—Most of the time we know when we have sinned with our tongue. How does this verse also help us understand the substance of our words when we're not sure?

DAY 3

In the first two days of this study, we looked at the right and wrong sides of our communication; comparing them with fresh and bitter water. Today we will look at the fountain of that water, the source of it: the heart.

Read Matthew 12:34-37.

18. According to the following verses, what emphasis does Jesus place on a person's words?

    verse 36

    verse 37

19. What circumstances, surroundings, or people cause you to think before you speak?

20. Even those who are the most flagrantly evil can produce the right words at the right time with a little thought and preparation. But in this passage, what does Jesus indicate is the significance of our "careless" words, the words that roll off our tongue, when we haven't prepared?

21. Verse 34—Why are our words a telescope into our hearts?

22. From memory, write the verse you memorized on "holiness."

23. Matthew 12:35—Will a person of holiness have to think before he or she speaks? Explain.

24. From memory, write the verse you memorized on "thought life."

25. Proverbs 17:20—Why do our thoughts, our words, and our hearts go hand in hand?

26. Ask God to bring to mind some of your specific words during the past 24 hours. What do these words reveal about you?

DAY 4

Today we will look at how sin of the tongue manifests itself in the form of gossip or slander.

27. What do the following verses teach us about the work of gossip and slander?

    Psalm 50:19-20

    Proverbs 11:9

Proverbs 16:27-28

"Technically, slander is the communication of a lie about someone else. Even when the things we say are true, they can malign someone when we communicate them our of context or by not giving other truths at the same time."[5] —Jerry White

28. Why do you think gossip can become such an easy trap for Christians?

Read Proverbs 26:17-28.

"Like one who takes a dog by the ears" (v. 17).
"Like a madman who throws firebrands, arrows and death" (v. 18).

29. It seems like the above phrases would be accurate descriptions of a child abuser or a murderer. Yet what do you discover in verses 17-19?

30. Verses 20-21—What do these verses teach you about the one who gossips?

31. Verse 22—How does this verse describe the words of gossip?

32. What do you think this means for the one who listens to gossip?

33. Sometimes we "spiritualize" our gossip. We take in the dainty morsels of rumors, half truths, and even mere information under the guise of Christian love, prayer requests, and a seeming desire to help. But how do verses 23-25 reveal what is often really true?

"He who conceals hatred has lying lips,
and he who spreads slander is a fool" (Prov. 10:18).

34. How do you think a person can know when he or she is gossiping?

35. Proverbs 26:26-27—How do these verses warn the person who gossips?

36. Proverbs 20:19—What is the warning here and why?

"When two people or two groups are at odds, gossip keeps reminding both sides of their problems. Gossip doesn't bring a balanced perspective or a reminder of the other side's good qualities. It feeds the quarrel with bite-sized reminders of bad qualities, bad decisions, bad reputations. Quarrels otherwise tend to wind down, because people get distracted and have other concerns to worry about. Gossip keeps them stoked up."[6] —Tim Stafford

Perhaps you have been the victim of gossip. Is there anything more harmful? King David had experienced its sting and wrote some verses in a psalm that we all can relate to.

Read Psalm 109:1-5.

37. Verses 2-5—What specifically happened to David here?

38. When could this have been your theme?

39. What was or could have been your initial response to this?

40. Verses 4-5—What did David do in the face of such injustice against himself?

41. What applications can you draw from this?

DAY 5

42. From memory, write the verse you memorized on "self-control."

43. How do the following verses encourage self-control in regard to the tongue?

Psalm 39:1

Proverbs 4:24

Proverbs 17:14

44. According to the following verses, how is the one who disciplines his or her tongue rewarded?

Proverbs 12:14

Proverbs 13:3

Proverbs 16:13

Proverbs 21:23

45. From memory, write the verse you memorized on "the new life."

46. As we have discovered, the new life consists not only of putting aside the bad, but also taking in the good. It is not enough to guard our tongues from evil, we must also speak forth that which is godly. According to the following verses, what type of speech should we hear from those who pursue Christlikeness?

Psalm 35:28

Proverbs 8:6

Proverbs 10:13

Proverbs 12:17

47. Proverbs 25:11—What do you think this verse indicates about the timing of appropriate words?

48. Circle the ingredients below that will always characterize words spoken in right circumstances.

Humor	Truth	Sensitivity	Fancy vocabulary
Courage	Eloquence	Prayer	Encouragement
Kindness	Warm tone	Religious	Genuine concern

49. Recall a time when someone's words ministered to you, gave you a new perspective, or set you on the right path. Describe this in the space below.

50. What ingredients from question 48 were used in this situation? Write them below and add other ingredients as well.

"A man has joy in an apt answer, and how delightful is a timely word!" (Prov. 15:23).

51. According to the following verses, how do timely words benefit the hearer?

Proverbs 12:18

Proverbs 12:25

Proverbs 15:7

Proverbs 16:24

Proverbs 27:9

52. What are your greatest needs in regard to your speech?

As you give these areas to the Lord right now, pray the following:

"Let the words of my mouth and the meditation of my heart be acceptable in Thy sight, Lord, my rock and my Redeemer" (Ps. 19:14).

[1] Taken from *Devotions for Growing Strong in the Seasons of Life*. Copyright © 1983 by Charles Swindoll, Inc. Used by permission of Zondervan Publishing House.

[2] Charles H. Spurgeon, *Morning and Evening* (Nashville: Thomas Nelson Publishers, 1994), November 29 entry, morning.

[3] Taken from *Basic Discipleship* by Floyd McClung. © 1988, 1990 by Floyd McClung. Used with permission from InterVarsity Press, P.O. Box 1400, Downers Grove, IL 60515.

[4] A. W. Tozer, *Faith Beyond Reason* (Camp Hill, Pennsylvania: Christian Publications, 1989), 79-80.

[5] Reprinted from *Honesty, Morality and Conscience*. © 1978 by Jerry White. Used by permission of NavPress, Colorado Springs, CO. All rights reserved.

[6] Taken from *That's Not What I Meant!* by Tim Stafford. Copyright © 1995 by Tim Stafford. Used by permission of Zondervan Publishing House.

WEEK 17
CHRISTIAN CONDUCT AND A GODLY DISPOSITION

DAY 1

The life of Jesus infiltrates every aspect of the believer. Our studies of Christlikeness have confirmed this to be true. As God re-creates the heart and mind, we emerge as changed individuals. This week we will focus on the outer manifestations of inward godliness and discover the potential of our conduct and disposition when we submit ourselves to the lordship of Christ.

Read 2 Corinthians 1:12.

"the testimony of our conscience"

1. What evidence is there in your life that you have a conscience?

2. What is the relationship between our conscience and our conduct?

Jerry White writes, "During an action the conscience is usually at its weakest level of influence. We become so involved in what we are doing that we are insensitive to the cries of the conscience. We may hear it, but rush forward with the action while making some weak rationalization in our minds. . .The conscience speaks loudest after an act has been complete, as it pronounces judgment on the act. Our conscience urges us to make restitution for the action. We can respond to this in various ways."[1]

3. It is one thing for your lips to testify about yourself or for another person to give a testimony about you, but how do these compare with the testimony of what your own conscience most often says about you?

"We can treat the conscience like a barking dog, tell it to lie down and be quiet, but it only slinks into the corner of our subconscious minds and gathers strength to bark louder later on."[2] —Leonard Griffith

4. According to today's verse, what did Paul's conscience testify about him?

5. From memory, write the verse you memorized on "a love for God's Word."

"For when Gentiles who do not have the Law do instinctively the things of the Law, these, not having the Law, are a law to themselves, in that they show the work of the Law written in their hearts, their conscience bearing witness, and their thoughts alternately accusing or else defending them" (Rom. 2:14-15).

6. It is clear from the above passage that the nonbeliever has a conscience. It is a conscience based on upbringing, instinct, and environment. But how do you think God sharpens the conscience of the believer as a more dependable source of conduct? (Question 5 may help here.)

7. What is a specific area in your life to which the consistent voice of your conscience has been directed?

Why is it best to heed this voice as soon as possible?

"Resist the temptation to participate in something because another believer's conscience seems to approve of it. Your conscience is the critical issue. . .If you don't have freedom of conscience to go to a theater, don't go even though a fellow believer has the freedom."[4] —Joseph C. Aldrich

DAY 2

8. From the world's standards, what makes a person "blessed"?

Read Matthew 5:1-12.

The teachings of the Beatitudes are some of the most profound in all of Scripture. Jesus begins His Sermon on the Mount with the basis of His value system. Today we will use these verses and discover the attitudes, dispositions, and behaviors that fashion a person for the divine kingdom, and we will contrast these teachings with the value system of the world.

9. Write what each of the following verses reveals.

A. Matthew 5:3: Poor in spirit

Revelation 3:17: The attitude of the rich

B. Matthew 5:4: Those who mourn

Job 20:4-5: The joy of the wicked

C. Matthew 5:5: The gentle

Psalm 37:9-10: Evildoers

D. Matthew 5:6: Those who hunger and thirst for righteousness

Ecclesiastes 5:10: Those who hunger and thirst for material possessions

E. Matthew 5:7: The merciful

Matthew 6:15: The unforgiving

F. Matthew 5:8: The pure in heart

Job 21:7,13-14: The wicked

G. Matthew 5:9: The peacemakers

Galatians 5:19-21: Those who participate in the deeds of the flesh

H. Matthew 5:10-12: Those who have been persecuted for the gospel

James 4:4: Those who make themselves a friend to the world

> "It should be noticed that this 'recipe' for happy and constructive living is of universal application. It cuts across differences of temperament and variations in capacity. It outlines the kind of character which is possible for any man, gifted or relatively ungifted, strong or weak, clever or slow in the uptake. Once more we find Christ placing His finger not upon the externals, but upon the vital internal attitude."[6]
> —J. B. Phillips

"God's kingdom turns the tables upside down. The poor, the hungry, the mourners, and the oppressed truly are blessed. Not because of their miserable states, of course—Jesus spent much of his life trying to remedy those miseries. Rather, they are blessed because of an innate advantage they hold over those more comfortable and self-sufficient. People who are rich, successful, and beautiful may well go through life relying on their natural gifts. People who lack such natural advantages, hence underqualified for success in the kingdom of this world, just might turn to God in their time of need."[5] —Philip Yancey

10. Look again at the beginning of the Sermon on the Mount (Matt. 5:3-12). Think about those things which Christ values (question 9). How does this challenge your own value system?

DAY 3

Read Philippians 2:14-15.

11. From memory, write the verse you memorized on "the tongue."

12. How do you know when a person's tongue has been infected with an attitude of grumbling?

13. How do you know when a person's tongue has been infected with an attitude of disputing or arguing?

14. How do you think such attitudes as those described in Philippians 2:14 will surface in a person's everyday lifestyle?

"Who is like the wise man? Who knows the explanation of things? Wisdom brightens a man's face and changes its hard appearance" (Eccl. 8:1).[7]

"It is almost impossible for a person to hide his disposition. If he is cold, critical, and severe at heart, it will come out in the little slips of the tongue, the defensive expression of the face, or even in his tone of voice. Many people seem to think that learning to be a good actor or actress is all that modern human relations demands. Believe me, to discerning people, acting is effective for only a short time. It is strange how slowly we learn that sincerity is the best psychology and that the way to win new friends is to be thoroughly true to the ones we already have."[8] —R. Lofton Hudson

15. How is the effect of a person's work limited when it is accomplished in a complaining or argumentative spirit?

16. 1 Thessalonians 5:16-18—What do these verses prescribe for the attitude?

What effect do you think these instructions would have on a grumbling and complaining spirit?

17. Philippians 2:15—As the obstruction of grumbling and disputing is removed, what will we become to the world?

18. Below, circle the areas over which you are most likely to grumble or argue.

Church	School	Uncontrollable circumstances
Home	Friends	Work
Health	Authority	Other

Considering what you circled, are you appearing as a light in the world?

19. What action must you take in regard to what you checked? (Refer to question 16.)

Make these actions a part of your life right now.

DAY 4

Read Titus 2:2-14.

"For the grace of God has appeared, bringing salvation to all men"
(Titus 2:11).

20. As God's people, what must we embrace. . .

. . .in regard to repentance (v. 12)?

. . .in regard to hope (v. 13)?

. . .in regard to the new life (v. 14)?

21. Read Titus 2:2-14 again and complete the chart below.

	Gender	Age	Specific Qualities Encouraged
verse 2			
verses 3-4			
verses 4-5			
verses 6-8			

22. Why do you think Paul encouraged specific qualities for specific age and gender groups?

23. According to the following verses, what are some of the results of such a lifestyle?

verse 5

verse 8

verse 10

24. "That they may adorn the doctrine of God our Savior in every respect." How do you think such behavior from believers (question 21) adorns or beautifies the gospel of Christ?

25. Which of the characteristics in question 21 help most in expanding your idea of godliness? Why?

26. Which of the characteristics in question 21 would help most in expanding your application of godliness?

Why?

DAY 5

Read 1 Thessalonians 4:9-12.

27. Verse 9—What does Paul say to the believers in Thessalonica?

28. According to verse 10, how were the Thessalonians acting on this love?

29. Verse 10b—What did Paul encourage them to do regarding love?

"By this all men will know that you are My disciples, if you have love for one another" (John 13:35).

30. Why is it so important that others see love in our conduct and disposition?

"For you yourselves are taught by God to love one another" (1 Thess. 4:9).

31. Though we will be cultivating a deeper understanding of the subject of love later in this book, how can you excel still more in your love for others today? (Let your answers be specific and active.)

32. At first glance, how do the words "ambition" and "quiet" seem to contradict each other?

33. Verse 11—Yet, how does Paul bring these words together?

34. How does this ambition differ from the world's ambition?

35. "And work with your hands." How do you think this can contribute to a godly life?

"As a result, people who are not Christians will trust and respect you, and you will not need to depend on others for enough money to pay your bills" (v. 12).[10]

36. As we discovered on Day 2, one of the key attributes most applauded by Jesus in the Sermon on the Mount was dependence—being dependent on God. But as we look at verse 12, we find that dependence in the context of today's passage may call our conduct into question to the outsider. When do you think dependence is evidence of a godly disposition, and when do you think it is not?

[1] Reprinted from *Honesty, Morality and Conscience.* © 1978 by Jerry White. Used by permission of NavPress, Colorado Springs, CO. All rights reserved.

[2] Leonard Griffith, *God in Man's Experience* (Waco, Texas: Word Books, 1968), 68.

[3] Charles Stanley, *The Wonderful Spirit Filled Life* (Nashville: Thomas Nelson, 1992), 191.

[4] Excerpted from *Gentle Persuasion,* © by Joseph C. Aldrich, (Multnomah Publishers Inc., Sisters, OR). Used by permission.

[5] Taken from *The Jesus I Never Knew* by Philip Yancey. Copyright © 1995 by Philip Yancey. Used by permission of Zondervan Publishing House.

[6] J. B. Phillips, *Your God Is Too Small* (New York: Macmillan Publishing, 1961, 1979), 107.

[7] *The Student Bible, New International Version* (Grand Rapids, Michigan: Zondervan Bible Publishers, 1986).

[8] R. Lofton Hudson, *The Religion of a Mature Person* (Nashville: Broadman Press, 1952), 115.

[9] A. W. Tozer, *The Root of Righteousness* (Camp Hill, Pennsylvania: Christian Publications, 1955, 1986), 123.

[10] *The Living Bible* (Wheaton Illinois: Tyndale House Publishers, 1971, 1973).

WEEK 18
PATIENCE, KINDNESS, GOODNESS

SCRIPTURE MEMORY
Your Choice
■ Pick a verse from this study to memorize and assign a topic to it.

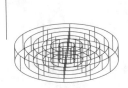

DAY 1

The writers of Scripture take every opportunity to enlighten us in regard to godliness and Christian character. This week we will focus on a passage of Scripture that is one of the most familiar in the Christian life. It is Galatians 5:22-23.

"But the fruit of the Spirit is love, joy, peace, patience, kindness, goodness, faithfulness, gentleness, self control; against such things there is no law."

Notice that Paul does not list these as the "fruits of the Spirit" but rather the "fruit of the Spirit." You don't possess one fruit without the others. They all go together. They all come from one Source.

John W. Sanderson also emphasizes this point. He writes, "Christian character is of one piece, and inevitably one trait will blend into another under close examination."[1]

We must keep in mind the context of all the fruit, even as we focus on a portion of them. We have already examined self-control. And by the end of this study, we will have analyzed them all. This week we will look at the fruit of the Spirit that describe how we must relate to other people: with patience, kindness, and goodness. It will be set up as three mini-studies, with an introduction and a conclusion.

The best way to understand the fruit of the Spirit is to understand the Source. So we will use our introduction as an opportunity to look at patience, kindness, and goodness in the nature of God and how He relates to us.

"Or do you think lightly of the riches of His kindness and forbearance and patience, and knowing that the kindness of God leads you to repentance?" (Rom. 2:4).

1. What do the following verses reveal to us about the nature of God?

Exodus 34:6

Psalm 86:5,15

Psalm 103:8

Read Ephesians 2:4-7.

2. Verses 4 and 7—What do we learn about His nature when we observe how He deals with us?

3. According to verse 5, in what state did our transgressions leave us?

4. Verses 5-6—How does His kindness and goodness literally lift us out of despair?

5. Read Isaiah 30:18. How does God's patience also allow for His justice?

6. Though our human nature longs for justice, what is the longing of God's nature?

When we exhibit the fruit of the Spirit in our lives, it goes beyond the little niceties and good manners with which we get by in the social realm. These may leave a good feeling or impression of us, but they do not leave another person with God. In the next few days may we truly come to understand and embrace the nature of God Himself in how we demonstrate patience, kindness, goodness in the world.

"How blessed are all those who long for Him" (Isa. 30:18).

7. How has today's study created within you a longing for God?

"God's long-suffering must be understood against the background of wrath and a day of reckoning. Long-suffering does not mean in itself that the basis for anger has been removed. . .It stresses the fact that a reckoning has been made and that wrath is deserved, but it is being withheld."[2] —John W. Sanderson

DAY 2

Read James 5:7-11.

8. Verse 7—What do a farmer and his crops teach us about patience?

9. "Be patient, therefore, brethren, until the coming of the Lord." James acknowledges here that patience is needed in waiting on the Lord's

return. What other aspects of your relationship with God could benefit from patience?

10. According to the following verses, what are the rewards or promises of waiting on the Lord? (Some Bible translations may use the word "hope.")

    Psalm 25:3

    Psalm 40:1

    Isaiah 40:31

11. Waiting on the Lord is an issue of faith. It is allowing God to have control of a situation. When you choose not to wait on the Lord, you choose unbelief. Who takes control then? Explain.

12. James 5:9—What else needs to be the object of our patience?

13. Which scenarios are you most likely to allow to test your patience? When someone. . .

___doesn't follow through with what he or she promised you
___keeps you on hold on the telephone
___is negative and whiny
___drives slowly
___is incompetent or catches on slowly
___wants to be around you and you don't want them to be
___is impatient
___sins

Fred M. Wood writes, "One of the truest marks of greatness is tolerance of a weaker person."[4]

"And we urge you, brethren, admonish the unruly, encourage the faint-hearted, help the weak, be patient with all men" (1 Thess. 5:14).

14. Sometimes we determine that someone is patient when he or she is easy-going or even lazy. This is not the genuine fruit of patience. According to 1 Thessalonians 5:14, when will you know that the real fruit of patience has been cultivated in your life?

15. From memory, write the verse you memorized on "endurance."

16. When you consider James 5:10-11 and the verse you wrote above, how do you think endurance relates to patience?

"But even if you should suffer for the sake of righteousness, you are blessed" (1 Pet. 3:14).
"Behold, we count those blessed who endure" (Jas. 5:11).

17. Think of a time when you or a friend suffered or were criticized for doing the right thing. How did God honor that patient endurance with a blessing?

DAY 3

Kindness and goodness are often difficult to distinguish from one another. And indeed they are closely related. But when Paul lists the fruit of the Spirit in Galatians 5:22-23, he differentiates between the two by recording them separately. Jerry Bridges help us to understand the significance of this. He writes,

"Kindness and goodness are so closely related that they are often used interchangeably. . .Kindness is a sincere desire for the happiness of others; goodness is the activity calculated to advance that happiness. Kindness is the inner disposition created by the Holy Spirit that causes us to be sensitive to the needs of others, whether physical, emotional, or spiritual. Goodness is kindness in action—words and deeds."[5] —Jerry Bridges

19. The fruit of kindness helps us to sympathize with others. It puts us in the shoes of our friends and helps us to see things from their perspective. It makes us sensitive to what they are experiencing. According to the following verses, what types of situations call for such kindness on our part?

Romans 12:15

1 Corinthians 12:26

20. From your observations, when is extending kindness more difficult: when someone is mourning or when someone is rejoicing? Explain.

21. How do you think kindness to others relates to sensitivity to others?

"For the despairing man there should be kindness from his friend;
Lest he forsake the fear of the Almighty'" (Job 6:14).

22. " 'For the despairing man there should be kindness from his friend.' " People despair when they feel like they have lost all hope.

What are some things a person can do to lift a friend out of despair? (Remember also question 4.)

23. How does what you just wrote help you understand what kindness is?

24. " 'Lest he forsake the fear of the Almighty.' " How do you think a person in despair might be vulnerable in his or her relationship to God?

25. Explain why kindness from believers is crucial at such a time.

"A friend loves at all times, and a brother is born for adversity" (Prov. 17:17).

When a believer observes that someone is despairing, facing adversity, or suffering in some other way, it is kindness that prompts the inner person to aid in the situation rather than taking on the attitude, "It's not my problem."

26. Yet, what may appear as kindness on the outside may not be the kindness that originates in the Holy Spirit. When do you think kindness could be used for selfish reasons to manipulate someone else?

Read Matthew 5:38-42.

27. It is one thing to extend kindness to those we love, to those who are helpless, and to those who respond in gratitude. But after reading the standards set forth in this passage, when will we know that our kindness is something that could only come from God?

"Our relations with other people are an indicator of our own spiritual health. Where there is unkindness, there is something wrong inside."[6]
—John W. Sanderson

DAY 4

The fruit of goodness seems to encompass a broad scope of examples. Shouldn't we know when something is good? Goodness is the opposite of badness, so we can base our definition on this—right? Yet even in Jesus' day it was not always that easy. There were times when those who opposed and hated Him criticized His good actions and attributed them to an evil source (see Matt. 12:24). The same confusion exists today. The same opposition exists today.

28. If non-Christian friends were to say of you, "He's too good to hang around us," would you take that as a compliment? Why or why not?

29. How does this encourage or discourage you to be good?

30. Psalm 37:27-29—Regardless of the world's opinions, why is goodness a fruit to cultivate in your life?

31. From memory, write the verse you memorized on "the believer's life."

32. Ephesians 2:10—What is the purpose of the new life?

33. "We are His workmanship." A table saw is used for cutting wood down to size. A hammer is fashioned for driving nails. Sandpaper is made for smoothing the wood. All of these tools were created with a unique purpose in mind. According to Ephesians 2:10 and 2 Timothy 2:21, how are we like these tools?

34. After a piece of beautiful woodwork has been created, who receives the praise, the tools or the craftsman?

"Goodness does not have to be publicized or paraded. It does not need a public relations program. Goodness is its own best advertisement."[7]
—W. Phillip Keller

35. What would be the absurdity of tools that agreed to be used by the craftsman only when the good work was something "important"?

What would be the absurdity of tools that agreed to be used by the craftsman only on Saturday afternoons?

36. How do questions 34 and 35 help you distinguish between the good works of the world and the good works that originate in the Holy Spirit?

37. Matthew 10:42—How does this verse encourage you to do good in the small things?

"It is one thing to do good in a few, or even in a number of isolated instances; it is quite another to face cheerfully the prospect of doing some particular deed of goodness day in and day out for an interminable period of time, particularly if those deeds are taken for granted by the recipients. But true goodness does not look to the recipients, nor even to the results, of its deeds for its reward. It looks to God alone, and, finding his smile of approval, it gains the needed strength to carry on."[8] —Jerry Bridges

38. From memory, write the verse you memorized on "time."

39. Galatians 6:10—What is a wise use of you time?

40. Where does the fruit of goodness place its priority?

Why do you think this is so?

"So that you may walk in a manner worthy of the Lord, to please Him in all respects, bearing fruit in every good work and increasing in the knowledge of God" (Col. 1:10).

DAY 5

"God's supportive presence makes every aspect of your caring relationships distinctively Christian from the start. . . . Jesus Christ does not stand on the sidelines waiting for us to use the right signal words for him to step in and be there. Rather, he is already in the middle of the situation. He's only waiting for us to see that."[9] —Kenneth C. Haugk

Read Luke 6:31-36.

41. Verse 31—Why is this a good place to begin in determining how much patience, kindness, and goodness to extend to others?

42. As you consider verses 32-34, how do our actions often rewrite the Golden Rule recorded in verse 31?

43. Do such actions (vv. 32-34) require any help from God? Explain.

44. Verse 35—Why is this Christlikeness at its best?

45. Think of someone who might fall under the category of an enemy for you. How might God use this situation to allow you to experience and demonstrate patience, kindness, goodness in a way you never have before?

46. What insights from this week will be the most helpful for you the next time you are face-to-face with this person?

[1] John W. Sanderson, *The Fruit of the Spirit* (Phillipsburg, New Jersey: Presbyterian and Reformed Publishing Company, 1984, 1985), 98. Used by permission.

[2] Ibid.

[3] David L. Hocking, *The Nature of God in Plain Language* (Waco, Texas: Word Books, 1984), 168.

[4] Fred M. Wood, *Hosea: Prophet of Reconciliation* (Nashville: Convention Press, 1975), 100.

[5] Jerry Bridges, *The Practice of Godliness* (Colorado Springs: NavPress, 1983), 231.

[6] Sanderson, *The Fruit of the Spirit*, 101.

[7] W. Phillip Keller, *A Gardener Looks at the Fruits of the Spirit* (Waco, Texas: Word Books, 1979), 146.

[8] Jerry Bridges, *The Practice of Godliness* (Colorado Springs: NavPress, 1983), 241.

[9] Reprinted from *Christian Caregiving, A Way of Life* by Kenneth C. Haugk, copyright © 1984 Kenneth C. Haugk. Used by permission of Augsburg Fortress.

How much is your money worth?

WEEK 19
THE LOVE OF MONEY

SCRIPTURE MEMORY
The Love of Money
■ Ecclesiastes 5:10
■ Luke 12:15
■ 1 Timothy 6:17

DAY 1

As you begin this study, you may be curious as to how this topic relates to becoming Christlike. This will be clearly defined during the week. It is not enough to understand the characteristics that contribute to a godly life; they must be lived out from an undivided heart. For when greed rules a person within, " 'the worries of the world, and the deceitfulness of riches and the desires for other things enter in and choke the word, and it becomes unfruitful' " (Mark 4:19).

"Our big concern, often, is a career. We think about material things. But God is thinking about manifesting His Spirit in our lives, so that we can have peace, joy, patience, and the other fruit of the Spirit. We think about wealth; He thinks about wisdom. We think about power; He thinks about purity. We think about a career; He thinks about character. His thinking is totally different from ours because He is far more concerned about what we are."[1] —Russ Johnson

Read Hebrews 13:5.

1. "Let your character be free from the love of money." How do you think the love of money will defile one's character?

2. According to the next phrase in this verse, how can you know when your character is free from the love of money?

3. When a person's character is free from this, in whom is he or she free to trust and why? (See the last part of Heb. 13:5.)

4. According to the following verses, what becomes of a person's relationship with God when he or she is not free from the love of money?

    Psalm 10:3

    Matthew 6:24

5. Matthew 6:24—According to this verse, when a person loves money, money becomes the master. What do you think are the demands of such a master?

6. Considering what you just wrote, why is it impossible to serve God and money at the same time?

7. Jeremiah 6:13—What types of people surrendered to the lordship of money in Jeremiah's day?

Are we any less vulnerable?

"Therefore let him who thinks he stands take heed lest he fall" (1 Cor. 10:12).

"Almost nobody fears prosperity. We fear dishonesty, impurity, gluttony, jealousy, and the various sins of the flesh. But not prosperity. And yet . . . prosperity can be a bigger danger than other difficulties.

Prosperity is also a threat to a close walk with God. . . . If our primary goal in life were a close walk with God, it seems clear that we would stop the pursuit of riches for the sake of amassing wealth because wealth makes such closeness more difficult. Usually, however, we rationalize our pursuit of riches by saying we need to provide financial security for our family. Or we say that others may not be able to handle riches, but we can."[2]
—John Edmund Haggai

DAY 2

Today we will see money as an unreliable and deceiving master, and why its mastery over us is unworthy of our lives.

Read Proverbs 23:4-5.

8. What warnings does the writer give us in these verses?

9. Verse 4—"Cease from your consideration of it." It is one thing to consider something, it is another thing to become consumed with it. Why do you think wealth must not even be a consideration?

10. Verse 5—What does the word picture in this verse teach you about wealth?

"For riches are not forever" (Prov. 27:24).

11. Do you think it is only the rich who can be tempted to make wealth the object of their trust? Explain.

> **"Money wants to claim the loyalty and love that belong only to God, and it has the power to capture us if we're not careful. Money is a marvelous servant but a terrible master, and only a disciplined devotion to God can enable us to keep Mammon in its rightful place."[4]**
> **—Warren W. Wiersbe**

"Someone has described a modern American as a person who drives a bank-financed car over a bond-financed highway on credit card gas to open a charge account at a department store so he can fill his Savings and Loan financed home with installment-purchased furniture. May this not also be a description of many modern professed Christians?

Perhaps some may be thinking: Are we to have nothing at all for ourselves? The answer is NO. Christ is to be ALL and in all . . . If you buy the new car, the new home, the new furniture, the new gadgets, hold down two jobs, etc., for the glory of God—well and good. But if we didn't have to have such a high standard of living would we not have more time to pray? If we were not so intoxicated with travel, pleasure, vacations, and recreation, would we not have more time to pray? If we were not so enamored of sports and entertainment, would we not have more time to pray?[3] —Paul E. Billheimer

12. **Check the reasons below why you think people place their trust in money.**

_____ To quench an inner thirst
_____ To gain power
_____ To provide security
_____ To keep up with what others have
_____ To obtain freedom
_____ To acquire happiness
_____ To feel a sense of self-worth

"Why do you spend money for what is not bread, and your wages for what does not satisfy?" (Isa. 55:2).

Read Ecclesiastes 5:10.

13. **"He who loves money will not be satisfied with money." When you consider what people expect money to do for them (question 12), why do you think it still leaves them in want?**

14. **It may seem like the answer to greed is to pursue poverty. But do you think poverty in and of itself is the answer? Explain.**

15. **"He who loves money will not be satisfied with money." Let's consider the possibilities with the rightful Master on the throne: He who loves God will be satisfied with God. According to the following verses, why is this true?**

Psalm 145:19

Isaiah 49:10

John 4:14

DAY 3

We begin today's lesson with an excerpt from *The Screwtape Letters*. Screwtape is a fictional elder demon training his younger nephew, Wormwood, in the things of hell.

"My dear Wormwood . . . the word 'mine' in its fully possessive sense cannot be uttered by a human being about anything. In the long run either Our Father or the Enemy will say 'mine' of each thing that exists, and specially of each man. They will find out in the end, never fear, to whom their time, their souls, and their bodies really belong—certainly not to them, whatever happens. . . . Your affectionate uncle, Screwtape."[5] —C. S. Lewis

Read Deuteronomy 8:18-19.

16. Verse 18—What is true about any amount of money a person possesses?

What about the wealth of those who are rich?

The wealth of a nation?

17. "But you shall remember the Lord your God." Why does wealth often produce spiritual amnesia?

18. Read verse 19, then describe the step-by-step destruction of such forgetfulness.

"It is the blessing of the Lord that makes rich, and He adds no sorrow to it" (Prov. 10:22).

19. We have observed how Satan corrupts the blessings of the Lord. For instance, he destroys the marriage union of two people with sins of adultery, jealousy, deceit, and selfishness. What do you think are some examples of sins that we must guard against in regard to the financial blessings of the Lord?

"Every good thing bestowed and every perfect gift is from above, coming down from the Father of lights, with whom there is no variation or shifting shadow" (Jas. 1:17).

20. Why must we remember that God is the source of our wealth and not ourselves?

21. From memory, write the verse you memorized on "discipline."

22. What might be some practical things you could do to discipline yourself in the area of generosity? Think: "As I have freely received, how might I freely give?" Start with small things and go from there.

DAY 4

Read Luke 12:13-21.

Prior to the words from today's passage, Jesus had spoken urgent words of eternal wealth, including the conditions for eternal life itself (Luke 12:8-9). But when Jesus pauses, perhaps just to take a breath, someone from the crowd pleads with Him to settle a family rift over an inheritance. Jesus, perhaps annoyed at first by such pettiness, seizes the opportunity to teach on the subject of greed.

"'Beware and be on your guard against every form of greed'"
(Luke 12:15).

23. Why do you think Jesus is so firm about His warning against greed?

If we are to be on our guard against greed, we must learn to recognize the warning signs. We must understand what circumstances make us the most vulnerable to it. The parable that follows in today's passage gives us great insight into this.

24. Verse 16—What was true of the man's land?

How do you think prosperity or present wealth could make us susceptible to greed?

"If riches increase, do not set your heart upon them" (Ps. 62:10).

25. Luke 12:17—Whose counsel did the man seek?

What might have been other alternatives to this?

26. Verse 18—What did the man's own wisdom tell him to do?

What are some alternatives he could have done with his wealth?

27. When do our motives for obtaining wealth make us susceptible to greed?

28. Verse 19—What did he think his wealth could buy for himself?

    How does wealth often bring with it its own troubles and anxieties?

"For not even when one has an abundance does his life consist of his possessions" (Luke 12:15).

29. Verse 20—For what was his wealth unable to prepare him or promise him?

30. " ' "And now who will own what you have prepared?" ' " (v. 20). What type of person would have likely gained ownership of his inheritance? (Refer to v. 13).

When it is all said and done, is this what you want your life to amount to—people bickering over money you didn't need and didn't have time to spend? Do you want your bank account to be the lasting memory of your life?

31. Verse 21—How is our attitude toward money an indicator of our spiritual state of being?

32. How has today's passage challenged your ambitions and future goals? Be specific!

DAY 5

Read 1 Timothy 6:9-10,17-19.

33. Verse 9—The outcome of wealth seems to be security, pleasure, comfort and ease, yet what will one actually find along the path of greed?

34. "Those who want to get rich fall into temptation." Why do you think that greed can become such an easy trap for Christians?

35. From memory, write the verse you memorized on "hating sin."

> "If you are content with husks, you will be counted with the swine. Does the world satisfy you? Then you have your reward. Make sure you enjoy it. There will be no other joys."[6]
> —Charles H. Spurgeon

36. Verse 10—How does Paul emphasize the seriousness of sin in regard to greed and the love of money?

37. Verse 17—As you observe Paul's instructions to the rich here, what does he indicate will be temptations that the wealthy will face over and over again?

38. "Instruct those who are rich . . . not to be conceited." How might riches distort one's view of oneself?

39. How might riches distort one's view of others?

40. From memory, write the verse you memorized on "humility."

"Greed equates a person's worth with a person's purse.
1. You got a lot = you are a lot.
2. You got a little = you are a little.
"God's foremost rule of finance is: we own nothing. We are managers, not owners. Stewards, not landlords.
Maintenance people, not proprietors. Our money is not ours; it is his."[7]
—Max Lucado

"And from everyone who has been given much shall much be required; and to whom they entrusted much, of him they will ask all the more" (Luke 12:48).

41. 1 Timothy 6:18—What will the person pursuing Christlikeness understand about material possessions? (Refer also to question 40 and the above verse.)

42. 1 Timothy 6:17, "to fix their hope . . . on God." Why would we do well to remember who is sovereign over our wealth?

43. "Not . . . to fix their hope on the uncertainty of riches." Why would we do well to remember this?

44. "Not . . . to fix their hope on the uncertainty of riches." In your day-to-day environment, what is most likely to tempt you to fix your hope on riches and materialism?

45. How might the verse you chose to memorize this week help you overcome this?

46. 1 Timothy 6:19—When we loosen the grip of greed from our lives, what are we able to grasp?

---

[1] Russ Johnson, *How to Know the Will of God* (Colorado Springs: NavPress, 1976, 1981), 10-11.

[2] John Edmund Haggai, *Lead On!* (Milton Keynes, England: Word Publishing, 1986), 157. Used by permission.

[3] Paul E. Billheimer, *Destined for the Throne* (Fort Washington, Pennsylvania: Christian Literature Crusade, 1975), 53.

[4] Warren W. Wiersbe, *The Integrity Crisis* (Nashville: Oliver Nelson, a Division of Thomas Nelson Publishers, 1988), 106.

[5] C. S. Lewis, *The Screwtape Letters* (New York: Collier Books Macmillan Publishing Company, 1961), 98.

[6] Charles H. Spurgeon, *Morning and Evening* (Nashville: Thomas Nelson Publishers, 1994), evening entry, July 4.

[7] Max Lucado, *When God Whispers Your Name* (Dallas: Word Publishing, 1994), 68. Used by permission.

Why aren't you content?

WEEK 20
CONTENTMENT

SCRIPTURE MEMORY
Contentment
- Ecclesiastes 5:20
- Philippians 4:12
- 1 Timothy 6:6

DAY 1

Read Philippians 4:11-12.

1. Circle the areas below where you have experienced discontentment in the last week.

The weather	Your mode of transportation
Your dating life	The way others treated you
Your family life	The peculiarities of others
Your town	Your living conditions
Your clothes	Your physical appearance
Your health	Your age
Your school	Your personality

Last week's study challenged us in the area of financial contentment. But as you can see from the above exercise, our bank account is not the only area where discontentment makes its deposit.

2. **In today's passage, Paul wrote, "I have learned to be content in whatever circumstances I am." According to 1 Corinthians 4:11-13, what had been his circumstances?**

3. **Knowing Paul's circumstances and his perspective of those circumstances, how might his life stir your own curiosity if you could observe him today?**

"I know how to get along with humble means, and I also know how to live in prosperity" (1 Cor. 4:12).

4. **Do you think a person will find contentment in prosperity if he or she never learned contentment in poverty?**

   Do you think that a person will find contentment driving a new car if he or she never learned contentment with the old one or the lack of one?

   Do you think that a person will find contentment dating someone if he or she never learned contentment as a single person?

Explain your answers.

5. "I have learned the secret." Did Paul discover this secret to be (A) putting his energy into changing his situation, or (B) learning contentment in spite of his situation? (Circle one.)

6. It may seem as though Paul just needs a little ambition. How does Philippians 3:13-14 answer such a theory?

7. What was the object of his ambition? (Refer to Phil. 3:10.)

8. From memory, write the verse you memorized on "wholeheartedness."

9. Look again at 1 Corinthians 4:12-13 and Philippians 3:13-14. List the action words in these verses.

10. Look again at what you just wrote. Do you think that a person learns contentment by dozing or by doing? Explain.

Being content doesn't mean being lazy or ignorant. Content Christians want to share their blessings. It's like having a peace and confidence in the middle of the battle, not running and hiding from it.

DAY 2

Read 1 Timothy 6:6-8.

"But godliness actually is a means of great gain, when accompanied by contentment" (1 Tim. 6:6).

11. What kind of gain do you think Christians are often under the impression that godliness will bring?

12. What kind of "gain" do you think Paul is writing of here?

13. Why does "gain" without contentment often seem like a curse?

14. From memory, write the verse you memorized on "Christian conduct."

> "The focus of contentment is Christ, not contentment itself . . . one reason most people aren't content is because they are trying too hard to be. If we will preoccupy ourselves with Christ, our hunger for contentment—and a whole lot of other things—will be met."[1]
> —Tony Evans

> "In view of such strong biblical warnings against covetousness and the earnest exhortations of the New Testament writers to be content with what we have, we must take seriously the need to earnestly pursue contentment as a dominant character trait in our lives. It is not a spiritual luxury. Contentment with what we have is absolutely vital to our spiritual health."[2]
> —Jerry Bridges

15. **When do you think Christians communicate to the unbelieving world that godliness is more of a burden that a delight?**

16. **From memory, write the verse you memorized on "the love of money."**

17. **Consider the amount of energy we use to gain money or possessions. Describe the possibilities if we applied this energy toward learning how to do without.**

18. **How much time and energy would this leave for pursing godliness?**

19. **How does verse 7 remind us that we are merely visitors in the world?**

20. **Verse 8—Why would a visitor to any place be content with the things mentioned here?**

Does it seem like you are more than just a visitor in the world?

DAY 3

Read 2 Corinthians 4:7-10.

"'When you pass through the waters, I will be with you; and through the rivers, they will not overflow you. When you walk through the fire, you will not be scorched, nor will the flame burn you'" (Isa. 43:2).

"We are afflicted . . . perplexed . . . persecuted . . . struck down . . ." (2 Cor. 4:8-9).

21. **Isaiah gives us a word picture of hazards that come externally. Likewise, Paul also writes of hazards which afflict us externally. But what does he say in verses 8-9 to suggest that such affliction had not overflowed or scorched him internally?**

afflicted in every way, but not _____

perplexed, but not _____

persecuted, but not _____

struck down, but not _____

22. **What do you think becomes of a person who allows the fire of affliction, perplexity and persecution to scorch him or her internally?**

23. **How would you paraphrase 2 Corinthians 4:8-9 to indicate what is happening in your life today?**

24. **2 Corinthians 12:10—What had Paul learned as he walked through the fire?**

25. **Look again at what you wrote on questions 21 and 23. What does this teach you about contentment?**

"We've been surrounded and battered by troubles, but we're not demoralized; we're not sure what to do, but we know that God knows what to do; we've been spiritually terrorized, but God hasn't left our side; we've been thrown down, but we haven't broken. What they did to Jesus, they do to us—trial and torture, mockery and murder; what Jesus did among them, he does in us—he lives!"³ (2 Cor. 4:8-10).

"What they did to Jesus, they do to us . . . what Jesus did among them, he does in us" (v. 10).

26. **1 Peter 2:23—According to this verse, what did humanity do to Jesus?**

   How did He respond?

"What Jesus did among them, he does in us."

The same dignity, contentment, and endurance demonstrated by Jesus then, He perfects in us today!

27. **Isaiah 43:2, " 'I will be with you.' " How does the certainty of Christ's presence protect the inner person from bitterness and resentment so that contentment can rule in the heart?**

DAY 4

Perhaps one of the most difficult areas for contentment to reign is the relationship we have with our own self.

"If God had a refrigerator, your picture would be on it. If he had a wallet, your photo would be in it. He sends you flowers every spring and a sunrise every morning. Whenever you want to talk, he'll listen. He can live anywhere in the universe, and he chose your heart. And the Christmas gift he sent you in Bethlehem? Face it friend. He's crazy about you."[4]
—Max Lucado

28. If you could change anything about yourself physically, what would you change?

29. On a scale of 1-5, rate yourself in regard to how often you think about the way you look. (Five representing that you think about your appearance a lot. These could be either positive or negative thoughts or both.)

1	2	3	4	5

30. In what other areas relating to yourself do you experience discontentment? (These should be things which you have no control over.)

31. From memory, write the verse you memorized on "thought life."

Read Job 10:8-12.

32. Did God just throw some paint on the canvas of your human skin, or did He create a masterpiece? Explain your answer from today's passage.

33. What does this say about the way He values you? (Refer also to Ps. 139:13-14.)

34. You were created in the image of God. Why is contentment in yourself more easily cultivated when you find your reflection in the person of God rather than in comparisons with other people?

35. What do you think a lack of contentment in regard to self reveals about a person's relationship with or concept of God?

36. Verse 12a—In spite of his or her imperfections, what does a person with a healthy relationship with God understand?

37. "And Thy care has preserved my spirit." What can we learn about contentment from this statement?

"For he will not often consider the years of his life, because God keeps him occupied with the gladness of his heart" (Eccl. 5:20).

DAY 5

As we wrap up this week's study, we will discover how godly contentment finds its way into the most destitute of circumstances.

38. Over what recent anxieties have you lost sleep?

39. Considering what you just wrote, have you ever found nighttime to be the most susceptible to anxiety and discontentment? If yes, why do you think this is so?

Read Habakkuk 3:17-19.

40. Verse 17—Here Habakkuk describes the destitution that awaits the unrepentant nation of Judah. The Lord would use the Chaldeans to discipline them during the Babylonian invasion. How does the prophet describe what is coming?

You may have known those who have suffered great loss in their lives. But how many people have you known who have been left with absolutely nothing? It is possible for people to face such complete destitution, but it is not probable.

41. Verse 18—Yet even when it was immediate, what was the resolution of Habakkuk?

42. Read Psalm 100:1-3. What do these verses indicate will help a person hold to such a commitment?

43. Habakkuk 3:19—What becomes of a person with such commitment to Christ, even on the weakest days?

Read Psalm 4:6-8.

44. Notice the question and answer in verse 6. Perhaps the real question is this: When a person is in the presence of the Lord's light, is there any other good? How would you answer this question? Explain.

45. Verses 7-8—What is the world with all its riches and pleasures unable to do that the Lord alone is able to do?

"Disappointment is the law for all earthly desires; for appetite increases with indulgence, and as it increases, satisfaction decreases. The food remains the same, but its power to appease hunger diminishes. Possession brings indifference. The dose that lulls into delicious dreams today must be doubled tomorrow, if it is to do anything; and there is soon an end of that.

. . . These eager desires, transfer to Him; on Him let the affections fix and fasten; make Him the end of your longings, the food of your spirits. And this glad longing for God is the cure for all the feverish unrest of desires unfulfilled. . . . Quietness fills the soul which delights in the Lord, and its hunger is as blessed and as peaceful as its satisfaction."[5] —Alexander Maclaren

46. Verse 8—How will this week's study help you during the nights when you can't sleep and during other anxious hours of the day? (Refer to questions 38 and 39.)

[1] Tony Evans, *Returning to Your First Love* (Chicago: Moody Press, 1995), 209. Used by permission.
[2] Jerry Bridges, *The Practice of Godliness* (Colorado Springs: NavPress, 1983), 109.
[3] Eugene H. Peterson, *The Message* (Colorado Springs: NavPress, 1993, 1994, 1995).
[4] Max Lucado, *A Gentle Thunder* (Dallas: Word Publishing, 1995), 122. Used by permission.
[5] Alexander Maclaren, *Expositions of Holy Scripture: Psalms* (Grand Rapids, Michigan: Baker Book House, 1974, 1977), 254-255.

WEEK 21
ANXIETY

DAY 1

For most of us, anxiety surfaces in a variety of circumstances. Whether it comes from public speaking, deadlines, relationships, tests, or the unknown, anxiety is ready to make us feel nervous, out of control, and cowardly.

Max Lucado writes, "The German word for worry means 'to strangle.' The Greek word means 'to divide the mind.' Both are accurate. Worry is a noose on the neck and a distraction of the mind, neither of which is befitting for joy."[1]

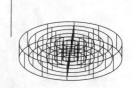

Read Matthew 6:25-34.

1. **Verses 25 and 34—Though anxiety may surface for a variety of reasons, what are the basic issues with which people become most preoccupied?**

2. **Verses 26, 28-30—How do the birds of the air, as well as the lilies and the grass of the field testify to the presence of God?**

3. **Yet, even in their own testimony of His presence, what limitations do you observe in their knowledge of and relationship with God, the very One who provides for them?**

4. **In light of this, how are you set apart from birds, lilies, and grass?**

5. **Verse 32—What are similarities that you share in common with the birds, lilies, and the grass?**

6. **Verses 26 and 30—What comparisons do these verses make between you and the birds, lilies, and the grass?**

7. **Why do you think the illustrations that Jesus uses in today's passage are so profitable in confronting anxiety?**

8. **Verse 27—Why is anxiety itself not profitable?**

9. What does Jesus say about the objects of our anxiety (question 1) in the last half of verse 25?

10. In the last half of verse 30, how does Jesus describe people who give themselves over to anxiety?

"And without faith it is impossible to please Him, for he who comes to God must believe that He is, and that He is a rewarder of those who seek Him" (Heb. 11:6).

11. Do you think that worry/anxiety is a sin? Explain.

12. Matthew 6:33—How might worry or anxiety be an indicator that something is wrong with our priorities?

13. From memory, write the verse you memorized on "wholeheartedness."

14. Write something that has consumed you with anxiety recently.

What would happen if you channeled this amount of energy into seeking "His kingdom and His righteousness"?

DAY 2

15. Describe the anxiety of the "what if's" or the worry of what could happen.

"The anxious man has a supply of anxiety stored up inside him; it may focus for a time on some acceptable object but, even if the object were removed, the anxiety would still be there."[3] —Leonard Griffith

Read Psalm 46:1-11.

16. Verses 2-3—What natural catastrophes are suggested as possibilities here?

17. What other natural disasters would cause you anxiety? Why?

18. Verses 6 and 9—What potential problems result in and among the nations unless God intervenes?

19. How does the threat of war cause you anxiety?

20. What other world issues cause you to experience fear?

21. What do the verses below say to indicate that God is bigger than any natural or human disaster or effort?

   verse 6

   verse 8

   verse 9

22. Where is God when disaster strikes?

   verse 7

   verse 11

"Cease striving and know that I am God; I will be exalted among the nations, I will be exalted in the earth" (Ps. 46:10).

23. " 'Cease striving and know that I am God.' " Why is this the best cure-all for anxiety?

DAY 3

Anxiety does not only center around our own needs and fears, but also in the hardships of those we love: the friend who learns of a close friend's abuse, the mother who watches her child being wheeled off to surgery, the son whose father is dying of cancer. Such situations are filled with anxious moments. We accept this as the natural response. As a matter of fact, we often consider this to be the spiritual response, thinking the more we fret over someone, the more obvious is our love and compassion for him or her. But actually, even in these situations the only thing that anxiety makes obvious is a lack of trust in God. Today we will look at how Jesus responds to the anxiety of a father in behalf of his son.

Read Mark 9:14-29.

24. Verse 17—What was wrong with the man's son?

25. Verses 18, 20, and 22—What was the outward evidence of this?

26. Verse 21—What did the father reveal here?

27. Put yourself in the father's place and imagine the day-to-day experience of such a situation. How would you feel?

28. What are some actions you might have taken through the years?

29. Verse 18b—What did the father do on this particular day and what happened?

30. Verse 22—" 'If You can do anything, take pity on us and help us!' " Considering what you wrote on the last three questions, why might it seem like the father would have a "right" to waver in his faith here?

31. Verses 19 and 23—Yet how does Jesus respond?

32. Couldn't Jesus have affirmed the father's concern for his son? Couldn't He have encouraged him in his endurance? No. It is faith that pleases God (Heb. 11:6)! It is faith that moves God. What must we learn from Jesus' response? (Read v. 23 again.)

33. Mark 9:24—How did one moment with Jesus confront all the years of lost hopes for the father?

34. Verses 25-27—And what happened?

35. Verse 29—Think of someone you really care about whose situation has caused you to worry. If you really care for this person's needs, what must you do?

36. Why are your anxieties and fretfulness over this person or anyone else a waste of time?

37. How do you relate to the father's plea in verse 24?

DAY 4

Read Hebrews 3:14-19 and Hebrews 4:1-11.

God promised Moses and the Jews that He would bring them out of Egypt. But this in and of itself was not the goal. The goal was to get into Canaan—the Promised Land. Canaan represented more than a geographical promise; it was a state of being, "that they should enter into His rest" (Heb. 3:18).

38. Hebrews 3:16—Who got out of Egypt?

39. Hebrews 3:17—What happened next?

40. Hebrews 3:18-19—Why did they not reach the goal of the Promised Land, which represented His rest?

But what about Joshua and Caleb who did believe? They indeed entered the Promised Land. For Joshua himself said,

"'And now the Lord your God has given rest to your brothers, as He spoke to them; therefore turn now and go to your tents, to the land of your possession, which Moses the servant of the Lord gave you beyond the Jordan'" (Josh. 22:4).

But as today's passage shows us, there was a rest beyond Canaan (v. 9). A rest that was not fulfilled in the Promised Land.

"For if Joshua had given them rest, He would not have spoken of another day after that" (Heb. 4:8).

In verse 7 the writer reminds his readers that many years after Canaan God still spoke of a promise through David yet unfulfilled. It was a promise fulfilled in the New Testament Joshua. Joshua is the counterpart of the New Testament Messiah, for the names Jesus and Joshua have the same meaning. Though Joshua was the Messiah of those who entered a geographical Canaan, the ultimate promise of God's rest is in the New Testament Joshua: Jesus. Only those who are in Christ rest beyond Canaan.

41. Hebrews 4:3—According to the first part of this verse, who enters the true rest?

Hebrews 4:1: "while a promise remains of entering His rest." So here is the goal of the Christian life, entering into His rest. This means that one experiences the calm, confident, victorious peace that God Himself enjoys. It is the disposition of God. His attitude and His very nature.

42. Do you see the nature of God as a place of rest? Why or why not?

43. According to the verses below, what prevents us from entering into His rest?

verse 2

verse 6

It is interesting that the very thing that brings us into His rest is the very thing which is most difficult for us to do. It is not our nature to trust; our nature is to question. This leads us to the anxieties and fretfulness of this life that we have discussed in this study.

44. From memory, write the verse you memorized on "discipline."

45. This rest is not the same as being saved, but rather it is the goal of those who are saved. It is our part to appropriate this rest through trustful surrender to Him. Why is anxiety the evidence of a disobedient life?

Christ makes this rest a fact of the Christian life. It is already yours. It has been accredited to you. Now may the facts of His rest become your experience from this day forward.

DAY 5

Today we will look at some passages hastening us toward the goal of resting in the Lord.

Read Psalm 37:7-8.

46. Verse 7a—How does this verse describe one of the aspects of resting in the Lord?

47. According to verses 7b and 8, what hinders such rest? Why do you think this is so?

Read Psalm 27:1-6.

48. Verse 1—According to this verse, how did David answer the anxiety of fear?

The anxiety of dread?

49. From memory, write the verse you memorized on "contentment."

50. Verses 2-3—Through what circumstances had David learned contentment?

51. Verse 3—How does he describe a heart at rest?

Verse 4 holds the key to such rest, not only in what David says but also in what he doesn't say. How many of us can say, "One thing I have asked from the Lord, that I shall seek"? If we were honest, we would have to admit that our prayers are usually more like this: Two things I have asked, Five things I shall seek; Eight things I have asked, Ten things I shall seek. We are content to make Christ number two, or place Him among the top three or four things of our hearts' desires. But the one thing? (Refer to question 12.)

52. Verses 5-6—Yet, what is He able to do?

53. Psalm 55:22—What does He replace your burdens with as you cast them upon Him?

54. According to Psalm 55:22 and 1 Peter 5:7, why can you trust Him with your burdens?

"God cares for you! Not only will He never leave you—that's the negative side of the promise—but He cares for you. He is not just there with you, He cares for you. His care is constant—not occasional or sporadic. His care is total—even the very hairs of you head are numbered. His care is sovereign—nothing can touch you that He does not allow. His care is infinitely wise and good." —Jerry Bridges

55. Philippians 4:6—What are the specific elements of casting your burdens on the Lord?

56. Philippians 4:7—And what kind of rest will you enjoy as you do this? (Refer also to question 42.)

Is this what you desire right now?

[1] Max Lucado, *When God Whispers Your Name* (Dallas: Word Publishing, 1994), 134. Used by permission.

[2] *My Utmost for His Highest* by Oswald Chambers. © 1935 by Dodd Mead & Co., renewed © 1963 by the Oswald Chambers Publications Assn. Ltd., and is used by permission of Discovery House Publishers, Box 3566, Grand Rapids, MI 49501. All rights reserved.

[3] Leonard Griffith, *God in Man's Experience* (Waco, Texas: Word Books, 1968), 40.

[4] Jerry Bridges, *Trusting God* (Colorado Springs, CO: NavPress, 1988), 199.

WEEK 22
JOY AND PEACE

SCRIPTURE MEMORY
Your Choice
■ Pick a verse from this study to memorize and assign a topic to it.

"The fruit of the Spirit is . . . joy, peace . . ." (Gal. 5:22).

DAY 1

"You greatly rejoice with joy inexpressible" (1 Pet. 1:8).
"And the peace of God . . . surpasses all comprehension" (Phil. 4:7).

Our flesh is incapable of fully understanding and experiencing the fruit of joy and peace produced by the Holy Spirit of God. As is evident from the above verses, even Peter and Paul were unable to find the words that would adequately describe the divine dimensions of joy and peace. If we hope to grasp them, we must go beyond what can be taught on paper, and ask the Holy Spirit Himself to reveal His nature to us in our own experience. May He use this study as His tool.

Read Romans 14:17.

1. Though the Jews centered much of their religious practices on their diet and observing the law in regard to specific foods determined to be clean, how does Paul describe the real totality of the Christian experience?

2. Why are we often tempted to place our confidence in our actions rather than in Christ?

3. Why do you think such deeds so often lack joy and peace?

"God's kingdom isn't a matter of what you put in your stomach, for goodness' sake. It's what God does with your life as he sets it right, puts it together, and completes it with joy"[1] (Rom. 14:17).

4. So, is joy and peace the result of something that you do or something that God does? Explain. (Refer also to Rom. 15:13.)

5. In what specific ways do you think we can make ourselves accessible to God that He may fill us with His joy and peace?

DAY 2

"'These things I have spoken to you, that My joy may be in you, and that your joy may be made full'" (John 15:11).

The words of Jesus in the above verse reveal a two-fold joy.

"'That My joy may be in you.'"
"'That your joy may be made full.'"

In the middle of inward anxiety, discontentment, and unrest, the soul longs for a deep, abiding joy. This is what Jesus promises to us. And not just any joy, but His joy—the same joy experienced by Christ Himself while on earth. He also mentions this in His prayer in John 17:13.

"'These things I speak in the world, that they may have My joy made full in themselves.'"

"'My joy made full.'"

Read Psalm 16:8-11.

6. According to the first part of verse 8, what produced the "glad heart" of verse 9?

7. What do you think it means to set the Lord continually before me? (Refer also to question 5.)

"Therefore my heart is glad, and my glory rejoices; my flesh will dwell securely" (Ps. 16:9).

8. Do you think that joy comes from the inside out or from the outside in? Explain.

"The joy of the Lord is your strength" (Neh. 8:10).
"My flesh will also dwell securely" (Ps. 16:90).

9. What do you think is the relationship between a person's joy and his or her sense of physical well-being?

"Neither wilt Thou allow Thy Holy One to undergo decay."

This passage is actually a prophesy concerning Christ long before His journey on earth. The joy spoken of here is, therefore, the very joy that Christ experienced through communion with the Father.

"Jesus said to them, 'My food is to do the will of Him who sent Me, and to accomplish His work'" (John 4:34).

10. "Thou wilt make known to me the path of life" (Ps. 16:11). What do you think is the relationship between joy and knowing and doing the will of God? (Consider also the example of Jesus seen in John 4:34.)

> "When the soul returns to its true home, when we find Christ as the way of life, when we relate ourselves to His will, joy springs up naturally in our hearts."[2]
> —J. Wallace Hamilton

11. Verse 11—Where does joy dwell?

Then where must you remain if joy is to indwell you? (vv. 8 and 11)

12. "Fullness of joy . . . pleasures forever." Considering these phrases from verse 11, to what extent may joy be experienced?

DAY 3

Today we will continue to look at the Spirit's fruit of joy.

13. Sometimes we think that joy and happiness are the same. But not so. Happiness is based on "happenings." If our circumstances are right then we are happy. Yet, according to the following verses, in what circumstances was joy present?

> "The Bible calls for joy as an abiding possession and a permanent state of mind for the saint."[4]
> —John W. Sanderson

Acts 16:23,25

Hebrews 10:34

1 Peter 1:6

"It is important, however, to distinguish between the joy of Christianity and what the world calls happiness. The New Testament talks much about joy but very little about happiness. And there is a difference between knowing how to laugh and knowing how to rejoice."[3] —J. Wallace Hamilton

14. Why can't we wait on our circumstances to make us joyful?

15. Philippians 3:1a—Rather, what should be the object of our joy? Why?

16. Philippians 4:4—How often should a Christian experience joy?

17. Philippians 4:4—Does this verse indicate that you must choose joy or that joy just happens? Explain.

18. From memory, write the verse you memorized on "hating sin."

19. In choosing sin, we reject joy. Why do you think this is so? (Ps. 32:3-4 may help.)

Joy is the atmosphere of heaven. Jesus makes it possible for you to live in that atmosphere moment by moment. Joy is His gift to you. It is your choice to take possession of it.

DAY 4

Notice the following declarations of peace.

"Glory to God in the highest, and on earth peace among men with whom He is pleased" (Luke 2:14).
This resonated through the heavens and the earth as the angels announced the Savior's birth.

"Jesus came and stood in their midst, and said to them, 'Peace be with you.' And when He had said this, He showed them both His hands and His side. The disciples therefore rejoiced when they saw the Lord. Jesus therefore said to them again, 'Peace be with you; as the Father has sent Me, I also send you'" (John 20:19-21).
These were the words given to the disciples following His resurrection.

As prophesied hundreds of years before His birth in Isaiah 9:6-7, Jesus came as the "Prince of Peace." His ministry on earth began and ended with peace. And today His peace reigns in the hearts of His descendants through the Person of the Holy Spirit.

Read John 14:27.

"'Peace I leave with you; My peace I give to you.'"

There are two types of peace suggested by Jesus' statement here.
- " 'Peace I leave with you.' " This is the peace of the conscience, the peace that comes from being right with God.
- " 'My peace I give to you.' " This is the peace of the heart, the peace enjoyed through the indwelling Spirit.

First we will look at the peace of the conscience.

"Therefore having been justified by faith, we have peace with God

> "Inner peace is a difficult concept to define, but it is easy to identify its absence. Like joy, it goes beyond mere emotion. And it certainly transcends circumstance. . . . Peace is an inner settledness."[5]
> —Charles Stanley

through our Lord Jesus Christ" (Rom. 5:1).

Read Ephesians 2:13-17.

20. **Verse 13—What was our position in relationship to God before we came to Christ?**

"For if while we were enemies, we were reconciled to God through the death of His Son, much more, having been reconciled, we shall be saved by His life" (Rom. 5:10).

21. **Ephesians 2:14a—How does this verse describe Christ Jesus?**

22. **"But now in Christ Jesus you . . . have been brought near by the blood of Christ." How does Jesus establish the "vertical" peace between God and man? (See Eph. 2:16.)**

   How does Jesus establish the "horizontal" peace between Jew and Gentile? (See Eph. 2:14b-15.)

Because we have peace with God through Jesus, we now can experience the peace of God through the Holy Spirit. This brings us back to John 14:27 as we look at the peace of the heart.

23. **John 14:27—Whose peace is given to us? What does that mean for you today . . . now?**

24. **How do the following verses describe the peace of the world, and those who only have this peace?**

   Psalm 28:3

   Isaiah 57:21

   Jeremiah 9:8

   1 Thessalonians 5:3

25. **What are clues that the peace characterized in question 24 is not the genuine fruit of the Spirit?**

26. **From memory, write the verse you memorized on "contentment."**

27. John 14:27—In the last part of this verse, how does Jesus describe a heart where peace rules?

28. What similarities do you see between contentment and inner peace?

29. John 16:33: " 'That in Me you may have peace' "—Why do you think a person will not experience peace outside of Christ?

How does this encourage you to seek a daily, personal, and abiding relationship with God?

30. " 'In the world you have tribulation.' " Jesus does not promise peace instead of tribulation. In fact He guarantees it. But He also promises peace in spite of tribulation. According to the last part of John 16:33, how is this possible?

"And the God of peace will soon crush Satan under your feet" (Rom. 16:20).

DAY 5

"And let the peace of Christ rule in your hearts, to which indeed you were called in one body; and be thankful" (Col. 3:15).

The Spirit's fruit of peace is not only evident in the inner person, but is manifested outwardly, too. Today's study encourages the cultivation of peace in our relationships with others.

Read Romans 12:17-21.

31. Romans 12:18—What is the Christian's responsibility in regard to peace?

32. How is it possible to be at peace with someone who is at war with you? (It will help to think of Christ's example.)

"It takes two to quarrel. If one of the two exudes good will, comes with good cheer, gives of himself in selfless love, that one is at peace. The other may still despise, hate, and abuse the first, but he remains the one with the problem, the one with the inner darkness and despair."[7] —W. Philip Keller

33. What are some principles of peace in the following verses?

verse 17

verse 19

34. From memory, write the verse you memorized on "the tongue."

35. "Never take your own revenge." When do you think our tongues become the tools of revenge?

36. From memory, write the verse you memorized on "thought life."

"Deceit is in the heart of those who devise evil, but counselors of peace have joy" (Prov. 12:20).

37. "Never take your own revenge." When do you think our thoughts become the tools of revenge?

38. Why must peace with others begin with our thoughts of them?

"So then let us pursue the things which make for peace and the building up of one another" (Rom. 14:19).

39. In pursuing peace with an enemy, it may seem like you are allowing him or her to hurt you and get away with it. According to Romans 12:19, why is this not true?

40. Verse 20—Anyone can be a peacemaker among friends, but when do our actions reveal that Christ is the Source of our peace-making efforts? Why?

41. How might such actions become the tools of a divine work?

To whom is God sending you to be a peacemaker?

[1] Eugene H. Peterson, *The Message* (Colorado Springs: NavPress, 1993, 1994, 1995).
[2] J. Wallace Hamilton, *Horns and Halos* (Old Tappan, New Jersey: Fleming H. Revell Company, 1965), 158.
[3] Ibid, 154-158.
[4] John W. Sanderson, *The Fruit of the Spirit* (Phillipsburg, New Jersey: Presbyterian and Reformed Publishing Company, 1984, 1985), 69. Used by permission.
[5] Charles Stanley, *The Wonderful Spirit Filled Life* (Nashville: Thomas Nelson, 1992), 183.
[6] Lloyd John Ogilvie, *Lord of the Impossible* (Nashville: Abingdon Press, 1984), 107. Used by permission.
[7] W. Phillip Keller, *A Gardener Looks at the Fruits of the Spirit* (Waco, Texas: Word Books, 1979), 112-113.

WEEK 23
COURAGE

DAY 1

SCRIPTURE MEMORY
Courage
■ Joshua 1:9
■ Proverbs 3:25-26
■ 2 Timothy 1:7

1. From your observations, how would the world characterize a person of courage?

2. What would you wish to add or take away from this stereotype?

Courage is not based on physical ability or strength; neither is it a momentary burst of bravery. Courage is not the absence of fear. After all, fear enables us to avoid the danger of sin. Rather, courage is moral character. It is the establishment of convictions rooted in the character of God and His care for us.

"Courage is an outgrowth of who we are. Exterior supports may temporarily sustain, but only inward character creates courage."[1] —Max Lucado

3. From memory, write the verse you memorized on "anxiety."

Read Proverbs 3:25-26.

4. "Do not be afraid of sudden fear." Circle the examples below which have at some time gripped you with fear.

Fear of failure	Fear of being different	Fear of others' opinions
Fear of death	Fear of comparisons	Fear of loneliness
Fear of Satan	Fear of physical harm	Fear of others' pessimism

5. Considering what you just circled, what crippling effect does fear have on people?

"Procrastination is usually the preferred alternative of the coward's heart. We all know that. When we leave the Lord's presence and power out of our analysis of a challenge, we will be gripped by panic and put off a crucial decision or action. What God has made clear in the light, we question in the darkness. Courage is fear that has said its prayers. Procrastination is fear that has forgotten what was promised in its prayers."[2] —Lloyd John Ogilvie

6. "For the Lord . . . will keep your foot from being caught." When we are faced with fear, verse 26 indicates that God becomes our Rescuer rather than removing our obstacle. Why do you think our depending on God allows courage to thrive?

7. Verse 26—What do you think is the relationship between courage and confidence?

"'And do not fear those who kill the body, but are unable to kill the soul; but rather fear Him who is able to destroy both soul and body in hell'" (Matt. 10:28).

8. When we fear the Lord, why is there nothing else to fear?

DAY 2

Read 2 Timothy 1:7.

"For God hath not given us the spirit of fear; but of power, and of love and of a sound mind" (KJV).

"For God has not given us a spirit of timidity, but of power and love and discipline."

9. How does this verse expand your concept of what courage is?

10. From memory, write the verse you memorized on "humility."

11. While it takes no courage to be timid, why does it take great courage to be humble?

"For you have not received a spirit of slavery leading to fear again, but you have received a spirit of adoption as sons by which we cry out, 'Abba! Father!'" (Rom. 8:15).

"Now we have received, not the spirit of the world, but the Spirit who is from God, that we might know the things freely given to us by God" (1 Cor. 2:12).

"For God has not given us a spirit of timidity . . ." (2 Tim. 1:7)

"For you have not received a spirit of slavery . . ." (Rom. 8:15)

12. Why would a slave have a manner of fear or timidity about him?

Likewise, how does Satan hold the world in fear's grip?

"Since then the children share in flesh and blood, He Himself likewise also partook of the same, that through death He might render powerless him who had the power of death, that is, the devil; and might deliver those who through fear of death were subject to slavery all their lives" (Heb. 2:14-15).

13. How have you been released from fear's grip? (Refer to the verses above.)

14. 2 Timothy 1:7: "Power, love, and discipline"—Why do you think that these are the expressions of true courage?

DAY 3

Read Numbers 13:1-3,17-33.

15. Verse 2—As the Israelites arrive on the threshold of the Promised Land, what does the Lord instruct Moses to do?

16. Verses 17-20—What did Moses specifically direct the spies to do . . .

. . . in regard to the people living there (v. 18)?

. . . in regard to the land itself (vv. 19-20)?

17. Verse 25—How long did this take?

18. Verses 26-27—What did they report to Moses about the land?

19. Verses 28-29,31—Yet, what seemed to be the emphasis of their report? Why?

20. Verse 32—In the final analysis, what did they end up reporting to all of the sons of Israel?

21. Verse 33—How did they compare themselves with the people of Canaan? How can comparisons cause fear and diminish our faith in Christ?

22. Verse 30—What was Caleb's perspective?

Read Numbers 14:1-10,22-35.

23. Verses 1-4—What was the consensus of the majority?

24. Verses 5-9—What issues of courage do you observe here?

25. Verse 10a—How did the darkness of fear persuade the people to respond to the faith of Joshua and Caleb?

26. Verse 24—How did the Light respond to faith?

27. Verses 22-23,34—How did the Light respond to unbelief?

28. There were 12 spies in all, "every one a leader among them" (Num. 13:2). Though they were considered the best their tribes could offer, only two came back with a report of faith. Why must we caution ourselves against listening for God's direction in the voice of the majority, the voice of human reason, or the voice of charisma?

29. How would Christianity today benefit from people like Joshua and Caleb?

DAY 4

Read Joshua 1:5-9.
In today's passage we read an excerpt from God's charge to Joshua following Moses' death. Though Moses had lead the Israelites out of Egypt to the borders of the Promised Land, Joshua was assigned an even more difficult task. Not only was he to lead them into Canaan, but also into battle against enemies superior to them in both number and skill. What words does the Lord choose to prepare a courageous leader for such an overwhelming assignment? What words would later play over and over in Joshua's mind when tempted to waver and disobey? As we behold these words, we gather from them sustaining qualities for godly living relevant today.

30. How does verse 6 reveal that courage was to be the character of Joshua's actions—what had God commissioned him to do?

31. Notice how often Joshua is urged to be courageous in this passage. Why do you think it is always linked with the word "strong"—"be strong and courageous" (vv. 6, 7, and 9)?

32. Do you think that such strength refers only to those with physical muscle? Explain.

33. From memory, write the verse you memorized on "a love for God's Word."

34. What words did the Lord use to address situations where fear might be an issue?

    When fear could be brought on by people (v. 5a)

    When fear could be brought on by the possibility of failure (v. 8)

35. According to the following verses, what were conditions for Joshua's success?

    verse 7

    verse 8

36. " 'Have I not commanded you?' " How would the certainty that God Himself had commissioned you with a task provide you with the courage to accomplish it?

37. " 'Be careful to do according to all the law.' " How does disobedience affect our courage to proceed according to His will?

38. " 'Do not tremble or be dismayed.' " How does this help us understand what courage is not?

39. If "courage" were to carry a banner into a physical or spiritual battle, what words from verse 9 would be on it? Why?

40. Over what area in your life do you need to place such a banner?

    Explain.

"What keeps us so cautious and afraid is our warped concept of success. Some people cannot act because they are so afraid of what might happen if they fail. They are constantly afraid of what others will think. Their concept of success is measured only by what they see and what they are told, not by what they are. But as someone wise once said, 'I don't know what success is, but I know what failure is. Failure is trying to please everybody.' "[5]
—Tim Hansel

Tomorrow we will observe a soldier who made this his banner on the front lines and in the heat of battle.

DAY 5

Read Judges 7:1-25.

41. Verse 3—After doing some simple math, how many men assembled in the beginning to fight the Midianites and Amalekites?

42. Verse 3—Why did the 22,000 men return home?

43. Verse 4—What does the Lord reveal about the 10,000 who remained?

44. Verses 4-6—What test does the Lord use to reveal His selection of warriors?

45. Verse 6—How many soldiers did Gideon end up with?

46. Verse 12—What was the number of the enemy?

47. Verses 7 and 9—What did the Lord promise here?

48. Verses 13-14—How did the Lord further confirm this promise to Gideon?

49. Verse 15—And what was Gideon's response?

50. Verse 16—With what did they arm themselves?

51. Verses 17-20—What was their plan of attack?

52. Verses 21-22, 25—And what happened?

53. Verse 24—How was the Lord's promise fulfilled?

54. Verse 2—What was the overriding lesson in all of this?

55. From memory, write the verse you memorized on "endurance."

56. Whom do you most admire here, the thousands who came forward for the moment or the 300 who endured in the face of conflict and danger? Why?

57. What is the difference between one who possesses ordinary courage and one who is a true hero?

58. How does Gideon's life challenge your own character?

"But you, be strong and do not lose courage, for there is reward for your work" (2 Chron. 15:7).

[1] Max Lucado, *The Applause of Heaven* (Dallas: Word Publishing, 1990), 81. Used by permission.
[2] Lloyd John Ogilvie, *Lord of the Impossible* (Nashville: Abingdon Press, 1094), 92. Used by permission.
[3] King James Version, *The Holy Bible* (New York: American Bible Society, 1974).
[4] Charles R. Swindoll, *Living Above the Level of Mediocrity* (Waco, Texas: Word Books, 1987), 100. Used by permission.
[5] Tim Hansel, *Holy Sweat* (Dallas: Word Publishing, 1987), 120. Used by permission.

WEEK 24
INTEGRITY

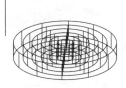

SCRIPTURE MEMORY
Integrity
■ Psalm 15:1-2
■ Psalm 51:6
■ Proverbs 10:9

DAY 1

It is difficult to pin down the meaning of "integrity" in a few words. This week we will look at the characteristics and the people that make integrity more tangible.

"Integrity is to personal or corporate character what health is to the body or 20/20 vision is to the eyes. A person with integrity is not divided or merely pretending. He or she is 'whole'; life is 'put together,' and things are working together harmoniously. People with integrity have nothing to hide and nothing to fear. Their lives are open books."[1] —Warren W. Wiersbe

"Integrity is a wholesome or moral completeness, and is characteristic of a person whose life reflects the life of Jesus Christ. Integrity demonstrates the inner person—the motive behind the act . . . Integrity encompasses all of what we do and are—speech, motives, and actions. A mature Christian walks in integrity, inwardly and outwardly."[2] —Jerry White

Read Psalm 26:1-8.

1. Verse 1—What did the psalmist's own integrity testify about himself?

2. Verse 2—Yet, whose evaluation of himself does he seek here?

"Behold, Thou dost desire truth in the innermost being, and in the hidden part Thou wilt make me know wisdom" (Ps. 51:6).

"If we want to be a person of integrity, we must begin down deep within us."[3] —Charles R. Swindoll

3. Psalm 26:3. "For Thy lovingkindness is before my eyes." How does being in the Lord's presence bring us face-to-face with who we really are?

"Many a man proclaims his own loyalty, but who can find a trustworthy man?" (Prov. 20:6).

"In this question of truthfulness, what matters first and last is that a man's whole being should be exposed, his whole evil laid bare in the sight of God . . . It is only because we follow Jesus that we can be genuinely truthful, for then He reveals to us our sin upon the cross. The cross is God's truth about us, and therefore it is the only power which can make us truthful. When we know the cross we are no longer afraid of the truth."[5] —Deitrich Bonhoeffer

"I have walked in my integrity" (v. 1).
"I have walked in Thy truth" (v. 3).

4. As Psalm 26:3 tells us, truth belongs to God. In fact, Jesus said He is the Truth (John 14:6). But verse 1 of today's passage suggests that integrity belongs to us. What do you think is the relationship between walking in His truth and possessing integrity within ourselves?

5. Psalm 26:4-5—What commitments had the psalmist made in regard to the godless people of the day?

6. God has placed us in the world and often around people with whom we have no choice of association. Yet, how is the company we keep by choice a true and strong indication of our character?

7. Verses 6-8—What was the psalmist's attitude toward worship?

8. How is our attitude of worship and church participation a true and strong indication of our character?

DAY 2

Read Psalm 15:1-5.

It is interesting that the word "integrity" is often used to describe inanimate objects as well as the character of people. For example, if you were discussing the integrity of a building, you would be referring to its structural soundness.

9. Verse 1 asks, "O Lord, who may abide in Thy tent?" Before we begin answering the question stated in the verse, let's first imagine the integrity or the structural soundness of the Lord's tent itself. What do you think it would be like—what words could you use to describe it?

10. Verse 2—How does the psalmist summarize the person who would be invited to such a place in regard to . . .

   • what he or she is.

"The average person has an amazing capacity for self-deception. In any situation he will face up to every truth except the truth about himself and will set the blame everywhere except the place where it belongs. Not many of us are prepared to accept the discipline of self-honesty. It involves a terrific strain. It can be such a forbidding experience, so utterly painful and devastating that we smash everything in sight before submitting to so terrible an indignity."[4] —Leonard Griffith

- what he or she does.

- what he or she speaks.

11. Verse 3—How will you know when integrity is lacking?

12. When a lack of integrity is exposed in one area of an individual's life, why might you question the integrity of other areas as well?

The integrity of a chain is tested at its weakest link. The integrity of a building is tested in its foundation, the part of the structure that no one sees. In what ways have you allowed the foundation of your life to become corroded from habitual unseen sin?

13. Verse 4—What characteristic will a person of integrity value in his or her friendships?

"He must not respect hateful people. He must honor those who honor the Lord. He must keep his promises to his neighbor, even when it hurts" (Ps. 15:4).

14. From memory, write the verse you memorized on "the love of money."

"He does not put out his money at interest, nor does he take a bribe against the innocent" (Ps. 15:5).

15. Does integrity have a price tag? (Consider the above translation of verse 5.) Explain.

16. How does the last half of verse 5 describe the person of integrity?

17. How does integrity prepare a person for his or her eternal dwelling place? (Compare what you wrote on questions 9 and 16.)

18. God has sent you an invitation to dwell with Him on His holy hill. It was an invitation in the shape of a cross and signed in blood. How does your life respond to His RSVP? Explain. (Refer to question 10.)

DAY 3

Read Nehemiah 5:14-19.

19. Verse 14—What position had been entrusted to Nehemiah?

20. Verse 15—What demands had the former governors placed on the people?

21. Verse 17—As governor, Nehemiah was expected to entertain important people at his table. Why do you think it would have been easy to justify his conforming to the practices of the former governors?

22. Yet, what did he not do . . .

    . . . verse 14b

    . . . verse 18

23. Why will a person of integrity, like Nehemiah, not be content with simply going along with the status quo, allowing the majority vote to rule his or her conscience and actions?

"Unless you can say 'No!' and do it very often, your life will be shattered from the beginning . . . unless you are in a very deep and not at all a technical sense of the word, 'Nonconformists,' you will come to no good. None! It is so easy to do as others do, partly because of laziness, partly because of cowardice, partly because of the instinctive imitation which is in us all . . . A great many of us adopt our creeds and opinions, and shape our lives for no better reason than because people round us are thinking in a certain direction, and living in a certain way . . . Truth has always lived with minorities, so do not let the current of widespread opinion sweep you away."[7] —Alexander Maclaren

24. From memory, write the verse you memorized on "Christian conduct."

25. Verse 16—In what other ways had Nehemiah demonstrated integrity?

26. Verse 15b—At first glance, Nehemiah may come across as boastful in what he writes, but where does he acknowledge that such actions originated?

27. Verse 18—What else motivated him?

28. What kind of pattern might Nehemiah's actions have set for governors who followed him?

29. What about your life? As a student, as a friend, as a believer, as a child under parental rule, how are you passing on the status quo of a conformist mentality in your actions and attitudes to those who will follow you? Write some specific areas where the world may approve or accept your actions, but where your own conscience is calling you to a higher level of integrity.

"A righteous man who walks in his integrity, how blessed are his sons after him" (Prov. 20:7).

DAY 4

Read Genesis 39:1-23.

In the not too distant past, Joseph had enjoyed a favored relationship with his father, Jacob, in Canaan—the land where his grandfather, Isaac, had sojourned. This favoritism had not gone unnoticed by his brothers, and they were more than unkind to him. Then, to add insult to injury, Joseph tells them about two dreams he had where each member of his family, including the brothers, bowed down to him. Their jealousy gets the best of them and they plot against Joseph to kill him. After they throw him in a pit to die, some Ishmaelites pass by and Judah, one of the brothers, convinces the others to sell Joseph as a slave. The brothers agree and lie to their father, telling him that Joseph was killed by a wild animal. Meanwhile, Joseph is brought to Egypt, where today's passage picks up the story.

30. Verse 1—Who is Potiphar?

31. Verses 4 and 6—What did Potiphar entrust to Joseph?

32. Verses 3 and 5—Why did Potiphar do this?

"The crucible is for silver and the furnace for gold, and a man is tested by the praise accorded him" (Prov. 27:21).

33. Verse 2, "He became a successful man." While poverty may test a person's faith, why do you think prosperity will test a person's integrity?

34. Verse 3—What must we remember if we are to maintain integrity in the middle of prosperity? Why?

35. From memory, write the verse you memorized on "temptation."

36. Verse 7—With what temptation was Joseph faced?

37. Verses 8-9—How did Joseph respond and why?

38. Verse 10—How did Joseph distance himself from temptation here?

39. What example does this set for you?

40. Verse 11—What opportunity presented itself?

41. Verse 12—What happened here?

42. What does Joseph's example in verse 12 set for you?

43. Verses 13-18—How did circumstantial evidence support a lie?

44. Verses 19-20—How might it appear that the cost of integrity was too much?

45. When has it seemed like the cost of integrity was too much for you?

46. Verse 21—Though Joseph's position and geography had changed, what had not?

47. Which would you choose, to be placed in a prison with God at your side and your integrity intact, or to remain in a mansion alone with a corrupted character? Explain.

48. Verses 22-23—How did God confirm that He was with Joseph?

"Faith's most severe tests come not when we see nothing, but when we see a stunning array of evidence that seems to prove our faith vain."[9]
—Elisabeth Elliot

"I have been young, and now I am old; Yet I have not seen the righteous forsaken, or his descendants begging bread" (Ps. 37:25).

DAY 5

Today we will look at integrity in the life of Daniel.

Read Daniel 6:1-27.

49. Verses 1-2—How did King Darius delegate his power in the kingdom?

50. Verse 3—Why had Daniel gained special favor with the king?

51. Verses 4-5—Though obviously envious of Daniel, what did the other commissioners and satraps have to admit was true of him?

52. Verses 6-9—Even so, what did they do?

Notice what is happening here and see if Warren Wiersbe's observation is true: "The person without integrity actually thinks that the darkness is light!"[10] —Warren W. Wiersbe

"And this is the message we have heard from Him and announce to you, that God is light, and in Him there is no darkness at all" (1 John 1:5).

53. Daniel 6:10—How did Daniel's integrity surface here?

54. Verses 11-17—How might it appear that the cost of integrity was too much?

55. Verses 20-24—Yet, how did Daniel's integrity allow his faith to become sight?

56. Verses 25-27—We know that Daniel honored God through his integrity, but how was it specifically used to glorify God here?

57. From memory, write the verse you memorized on "endurance."

58. How does this study encourage you to keep the candle of integrity lit even when surrounded by darkness?

"'Nor do men light a lamp, and put it under the peck-measure,
but on the lampstand; and it gives light to all who are in the house'"
(Matt. 5:15).

[1] Warren W. Wiersbe, *The Integrity Crisis* (Nashville: Oliver Nelson a Division of Thomas Nelson Publishers, 1988), 21.
[2] Reprinted from *Honesty, Morality and Conscience*. © 1978 by Jerry White. Used by permission of NavPress, Colorado Springs, CO. All rights reserved.
[3] *Strengthening Your Grip*, Charles R. Swindoll, 1982, Word Publishing, Nashville, Tennessee. All rights reserved. Used by permission.
[4] Leonard Griffith, *God in Man's Experience* (Waco, Texas: Word Books, 1968), 87.
[5] Deitrich Bonhoeffer, *The Cost of Discipleship* (New York: Macmillan Publishing Co. Inc., 1963, 1976), 155.
[6] *The Everyday Bible, New Century Version* (Dallas: Word Publishing, 1987, 1988).
[7] Alexander Maclaren, *Expositions of Holy Scripture: Nehemiah* (Grand Rapids, Michigan: Baker Book House, 1974, 1977), 362-363; 364.
[8] *Strengthening Your Grip*, Charles R. Swindoll.
[9] Elisabeth Elliot, *These Strange Ashes* (San Francisco: Harper & Row, Publishers, 1979).
[10] Warren W. Wiersbe, *The Integrity Crisis*, 23.

WEEK 25
FAITHFULNESS

SCRIPTURE MEMORY
Faithfulness
- Luke 16:10

"The fruit of the Spirit is . . . faithfulness" (Gal. 5:23).

DAY 1

1. Line up the following words or phrases under the correct heading below.

Unpredictable; Dependable; Trustworthy; Whimsical; Loyal; Traitor; Wavering; Disobedient; Wholehearted; Truthful; Steadfast; Infidelity; Fickle; Few words, much action; Many words, little action; Stable; Reliable; Dishonest.

An Outline of Faithfulness　　　　　　**An Outline of Faithlessness**

Now add any other words that come to mind.

"The man who is concerned only with himself and his own moral rectitude will not have a good reputation for dependability among his neighbors because his actions will be determined by the ebb and flow of his passing moods, not by his commitment to anything outside of himself."[1] —John W. Sanderson

Read Psalm 89:1-18.

2. Verse 2, "In the heavens Thou wilt establish Thy faithfulness." How would you compare the faithfulness of heaven with the "faithfulness" you observe on earth?

3. Verse 8, "Thy faithfulness also surrounds Thee." Imagine the word picture suggested by this verse. God is hedged in by His faithfulness; it surrounds Him. He cannot get away from it, nor would He desire to. What other attributes or characteristics of God can you find mentioned and/or indicated in the following verses?

verse 2

verse 13

verse 14

4. Verses 3-4—What covenant had He made with David?

5. Was this covenant based on David's faithfulness, his sons' faithfulness, or God's faithfulness? (Refer to verses 30-37.)

6. From memory, write the verse you memorized on "who you are in Christ."

7. What promises does He make to those who are in Christ?

Philippians 1:6

1 Thessalonians 5:24

1 John 1:9

8. Are these promises based on your righteousness or God's righteousness? Explain. (Refer to question 4.)

9. Psalm 89:1—How was the psalmist faithful in his verbal witness?

10. How is God's faithfulness and power seen in His creation?

verse 5

verse 9

verses 11-12

11. How do verses 15 and 16 describe the people who faithfully surround themselves with the presence of God?

12. Verse 10—How is God's faithfulness made evident in the way He deals with the enemy?

"But the Lord is faithful, and He will strengthen and protect you from the evil one" (2 Thess. 3:3).

DAY 2

Read Matthew 24:45-51.

13. Verse 45—What was the one task that the master entrusted to the slave in regard to his household?

14. In the first part of verse 45, how does Jesus describe this slave?

15. Verse 46—Why? (Check one.)

___ A. because of the slave's good intention
___ B. because of the slave's good education
___ C. because of the slave's good action

16. Verse 47—How did a seemingly insignificant responsibility prove otherwise?

17. Verse 48—How does Jesus describe this slave?

18. Verse 48—Of what was the slave able to convince himself?

19. Verse 49—And what did he do in response?

20. Verses 50-51—How did a seemingly normal day prove otherwise?

21. By removing his presence, what did the master learn that he would not have discovered if he had been visible everyday?

22. From memory, write the verse you memorized on "time."

23. In regard to the following, what has the Master learned about you by removing His visible presence . . .

your sexual activity

your tongue

the way you discipline yourself

your endurance

your conduct and attitude

your love of money

As you consider the above, do you resemble the faithful slave or the evil slave? Explain. (As you think through this, refer to question 15.)

24. **Verse 49—What becomes of freedom when a person becomes convinced of no accountability?**

25. **From memory, write the verse you memorized on "a love for God's Word."**

26. **How does our faithfulness begin with believing the words of the Master?**

27. **Verse 51—And what will become of us if we don't believe?**

DAY 3

Read Luke 16:1-9.

This is considered by many as the most difficult parable in the Scriptures. We are reluctant to learn from unrighteous men and even more reluctant to accept that Jesus would use an unrighteous person to teach us a lesson on faithfulness; yet, this is what He does.

28. **Verse 1—Why had the steward lost favor with his master?**

He wasn't able to dig and he wasn't about to beg (v. 3). So in his last moments as a steward, he comes up with a plan to make friends with those who were indebted to his master so that at least he would have a roof over his head (v. 4).

29. **Verse 6—Though the first debtor owed the master 100 measures (800 gallons) of oil, what would the bill now read, thanks to the adjustments of the unrighteous steward?**

Verse 7—Though the second debtor owed 100 measures (1,000 bushels) of wheat, what would the bill now read?

30. **Verse 8a—Though the steward was a crook, what did the master himself have to admit about his actions?**

"We have a habit of dividing life into compartments. There is the part of life in which we remember that God is present; and there is the part of life in which we never think of God at all. We tend to draw a line between the activities which are sacred and the activities which are secular. But if we really know what Christianity means we will know that for us there is no part of life when the master is away. We are working and living forever in our great task-master's eye."[2]
—William Barclay

Now for the lessons:

1) Fervor: Though the steward did what was wrong, he worked at it. He knew his days were numbered, and he gave 100 percent.

2) Foresight: He was able to look down the road and see more than what lay on the surface. He saw what would happen if he didn't act. He was also a man of vision. He saw the potential of his resources.

3) Finances: He used finances to make friends.

"'Yes, worldly people are smarter with their own kind than spiritual people are'"; (v. 8b).

31. From memory, write the verse you memorized on "wholeheartedness."

32. What areas of the Christian life would benefit from the fervor of the unrighteous steward? Why?

33. What areas of the Christian life would benefit from the foresight of the unrighteous steward? Why?

"'I tell you, make friends for yourselves using worldly riches. Then, when those things are gone, you will be welcomed in that home that continues forever'"⁺ (Luke 16:9).

34. From memory, write the verse you memorized on "the love of money."

Faithfulness in your use of money is revealed in how much of it is used to secure friends in heaven. Will people spend eternity in heaven because of the way you used your money?

35. When do we squander the Master's money on our own greed and desires?

We will return to this chapter tomorrow, and focus on one of the classic verses regarding faithfulness.

DAY 4

Read Luke 16:10-12.

36. Verse 10—When do you know that you can trust someone with a big task?

37. " 'He who is faithful in a very little thing.' " How would you define "little things?"

38. Why would this be a good testing arena for true faithfulness?

39. Why do we often consider such things (question 37) as unworthy of our time and efforts?

40. Complete the following sentence based on Luke 16:10: If I want God to reveal His will to me regarding the future, then . . .

41. Why must we be faithful to God in the situation we are in right now?

42. Verse 11—How is our handling of worldly riches an indication of how we will handle eternal riches?

43. Verse 12—How is our response in a position of service an indication of how we will perform in a position of leadership?

DAY 5

Today we will look at faithfulness in friendship.

"But Samuel said to Saul, 'I will not return with you; for you have rejected the word of the Lord, and the Lord has rejected you from being king over Israel.' And as Samuel turned to go, Saul seized the edge of his robe, and it tore. So Samuel said to him, 'The Lord has torn the kingdom of Israel from you today, and has given it to your neighbor who is better than you'" (1 Sam. 15:26-28).

Read 1 Samuel 20:1-42.

44. Verse 1—What did David fear according to the last part of this verse?

> "If we cannot serve God in the situation we're in right now, then what makes us think we can do better in a different location or position? The human tendency is to avoid the mundane and graduate to the spectacular, but that is not God's way. Godly character exemplified through the fruit of the Spirit can be as easily seen in small tasks as it can in large ones."[5]
> —Floyd McClung

45. Verse 4—What commitment does Jonathan make to David?

46. Verses 5-7—How does David ask Jonathan to "test the waters" with Saul on his behalf?

47. Verse 8—David thought Saul's motive for wanting him killed was because of some sin in his life rather than Saul's own jealousy. What does David ask of Jonathan here?

48. Verses 9-12—What commitment did Jonathan make to David in these verses?

49. What might have happened if Jonathan had vowed only to tell David what he wanted to hear?

"Faithful are the wounds of a friend, but deceitful are the kisses of an enemy" (Prov. 27:6).

50. 1 Samuel 20:13, "May the Lord be with you as He has been with my father." This is an interesting statement. Neither Jonathan nor David had been told that the Lord had rejected Saul as king. But what does Jonathan say in verses 14-16 that would indicate God had made it known to him that David would be the next king?

51. Verse 17—What does this say about Jonathan's commitment to David?

52. Verses 18-22—What plans did they come up with?

53. Verse 23—What does this verse reveal about their friendship?

54. Verses 24-29—What happened next?

55. Verses 30-31—How does Saul respond?

56. Verses 32-34—What happened between Saul and Jonathan?

57. Though Saul's words dishonored Jonathan (v. 30), what was the reason he grieved in verse 34?

58. Verses 35-40—How was Jonathan faithful to his vow?

59. Verse 41—What were the expressions of friendship here?

60. Verse 42—What was the reason that David and Jonathan had found such a faithful friend in each other?

61. What does the example of David and Jonathan teach you about what it means to be a faithful friend?

[1] John W. Sanderson, *The Fruit of the Spirit* (Phillipsburg, New Jersey: Presbyterian and Reformed Publishing Company, 1984, 1985), 116. Used by permission.

[2] William Barclay, *The Gospel of Luke* (Philadelphia: The Westminster Press, 1975), 172.

[3] *The Everyday Bible, New Century Version* (Dallas: Word Publishing, 1987, 1988).

[4] Ibid.

[5] Floyd McClung, *Basic Discipleship* (Downers Grove, Illinois: InterVarsity Press, 1988, 1990), 38. Used by permission.

Jesus described Himself as gentle

WEEK 26
GENTLENESS

SCRIPTURE MEMORY
Gentleness
- Matthew 11:28-29
- Matthew 12:20
- 1 Peter 3:4

DAY 1

Read Matthew 11:28-30.

1. Write the specific invitations extended by Jesus in this passage.

2. From memory, write the verse you memorized on "anxiety."

Both verse 28 and verse 29 emphasize the rest found in Jesus, but they are two different rests.

Verse 28—" 'Come to Me . . . and I will give you rest.' " This rest refers to salvation. When you asked Jesus to be your Savior and Lord, you entered into this rest.

Verse 29—" 'Take My yoke upon you, and learn from Me . . . and you shall find rest for your souls.' " This rest refers to the experience of the Christian life. This rest becomes yours as you share in Christ's life or abide in Him on a daily basis.

3. When He says, " 'Take My yoke upon you,' " it is as though He is saying, "Take My life upon you." How does He describe His life in verse 29.

The Bible records several instances when Jesus describes His purpose. But here He describes Himself. He could have described Himself as a mighty person, a forgiving person, a generous person. Others have described Him in these ways, and they are all accurate descriptions. But gentle and humble is the way Jesus described Himself. This is how He saw His own personhood.

4. Verse 29—" 'and learn from Me.' " What does Jesus say will become of the weary-one-turned-student?

5. How can you commit this week to sharing His yoke: learning from Him and abiding in Him?

6. Verse 30—What does He reveal here about His own curriculum?

Why do you think he describes it this way?

7. How has today's passage helped motivate you for a week of study focusing on gentleness?

DAY 2

To understand gentleness, we must look to Jesus, who purposefully described Himself as " 'gentle and humble in heart' " (Matt. 11:29).

8. From memory, write the verse you memorized on "humility."

As we keep the principles of humility before us, our understanding of gentleness will be greatly enriched. Humility adds the dimensions of lowliness and meekness to the overall scope of gentleness. These words are used often to describe Jesus.

9. What do the following verses reveal about the lowliness or meekness of Christ? Complete the following sentences based on what the verses reveal.

    A. Though He could have been born in a palace . . . (Luke 2:7)

    B. Though He had all authority . . . (Luke 2:51)

    C. Though He could have been served . . . (Mark 6:3)

    D. Though He had the right to ownership of all things . . . (Matt. 8:20)

    E. Though death had no hold on Him . . . (Phil. 2:8)

10. 1 Peter 2:23—How does this verse describe the meekness of Christ?

11. What do the following verses reveal about the gentleness of Christ?

    A. In His treatment of children (Matt. 19:14).

    B. In the face of one who would deny Him (Luke 22:31-34).

    C. In the care of His mother (John 19:26-27).

12. Look again at what you wrote on question 11. Where does "gentleness" place its value?

13. Describe how gentleness is humility in action.

> Jerry Bridges writes, "Gentleness is somewhat difficult to define, because it is often confused with meekness, which is another Christian virtue that we should pursue . . . Gentleness is an active trait, describing the manner in which we should treat others. Meekness is a passive trait, describing the proper Christian response when others mistreat us."[1] —Jerry Bridges

"Gentleness includes such enviable qualities as having strength under control, being calm and peaceful when surrounded by a heated atmosphere, emitting a soothing effect on those who may be angry or otherwise beside themselves, and possessing tact and gracious courtesy that causes others to retain their self-esteem and dignity. Clearly, it includes a Christlikeness . . ."[2]
—Charles R. Swindoll

DAY 3

Read Matthew 12:9-21.

14. Verses 9-10—What motivated the Pharisees' question?

15. Verse 13—Yet, what did Jesus do?

16. Verses 11-12—What motivated His action?

17. Verse 14—For what purpose did the Pharisees act diligently?

18. Verse 15b—For what purpose did Jesus act diligently?

19. Verses 15-16—How did Jesus respond to what the Pharisees were doing?

Why do you think He did this?

20. Verse 17—What reason does Matthew give for Jesus' response?

21. Match the actions of Jesus from today's passage with prophecies spoken by Isaiah (see Isa. 42:2-3).

    A. verses 15-16—He withdrew and kept a low profile.
    B. verses 10, 13—He ministered to and healed the man with the withered hand.
    C. verses 11-12—He didn't quarrel.

_____ He will not quarrel, nor cry out
_____ Nor will anyone hear His voice in the streets
_____ A battered reed He will not break off, and a smoldering wick He will not put out

22. What does this teach you about gentleness?

23. Verse 20—" 'A battered reed He will not break off.' " If a battered reed is to be handled at all, how must it be handled?

24. Though you may have enough strength or power in your hands to break a fragile crystal glass, why would you want to handle it gently?

25. Verse 20—" 'A smoldering wick He will not put out.' " If a smoldering wick is to be approached at all, how must it be approached if it is to be prevented from going out completely?

26. From memory, write the verse you memorized on "hating sin."

27. When have specific sins in your life caused you to resemble a battered reed or smoldering wick?

28. A careless breath may extinguish a smoldering wick. A gentle breath may actually fan the flame. Remember the vulnerable time in your life you wrote about on question 27 and describe the breath that would not smother—the breath that would ignite even the most fragile of flames. Circle the words below that would describe such a breath.

Peaceful	Secure	Weak	Forgiving
Cowering	Hopeful	Passive	Sentimental
Patient	Distant	Protective	Wise

29. How do you know when the Holy Spirit is speaking to you? (Refer to question 28.)

30. What motivates the Holy Spirit to care for you this way? (Refer to questions 12, 16 and 24.)

31. Think of someone, a brother or sister in Christ, who could be described spiritually as a battered reed or smoldering wick. Why is the fruit of gentleness so important in the way you relate to him or her?

DAY 4

Read Isaiah 40:10-11.

32. Verse 10—"Behold, the Lord God will come with might, with His arm ruling for Him." Describe the strength of such an arm.

33. Verse 11—What does He do with His arm?

34. Verse 11—What does this word picture teach you about the gentleness of Jesus?

"And what man among you, if he has a hundred sheep and has lost one of them, does not leave the ninety-nine in the open pasture, and go after the one which is lost, until he finds it? And when he has found it, he lays it on his shoulders, rejoicing" (Luke 15:4-5).

35. Isaiah 40:11—The man in the above passage lays the once lost sheep on his shoulders. The picture of God we see in Isaiah is one who carries the lamb close to His heart. What subtle differences do you see here?

Read 1 Thessalonians 2:5-7.

36. 1 Thessalonians 2:5-6—What methods mentioned here can achieve a desired outcome?

37. 1 Thessalonians 2:7—How did Paul rise above these methods in his founding of the church at Thessalonica?

38. 1 Thessalonians 2:7—What does this word picture teach you about gentleness?

39. How would the following relationships in your life benefit from such an approach seen in verse 7?

Your best friend

A rival

A backslidden Christian

A non-Christian

An assailant

40. Do you think that a gentle response allows those who have hurt you to get away with it? Explain.

DAY 5

The world's value system doesn't encourage gentleness in anyone. The time has passed when the term "gentleman" would describe the best a man could be. It is no less a threat to today's definition of "womanhood." But the fruit of the Spirit goes beyond the classifications of gender.

"There is neither Jew nor Greek, there is neither slave nor free man, there is neither male nor female; for you are all one in Christ Jesus" (Gal. 3:28).

The same Spirit who gives love, joy, peace, patience, kindness, goodness, faithfulness, and self-control also gives gentleness. Men do not receive one fruit of gentleness, while women receive another variety. It is one Spirit who gives to all. Today we will further see how gentleness is manifested in each of us.

41. 1 Timothy 6:11—What does Paul write about gentleness in regard to men?

   1 Peter 3:4—What does Peter write about gentleness in regard to women?

42. How would Christlikeness be manifested more fully in you if you applied the principles of both verses to your own life?

43. From memory, write the verse you memorized on "courage."

44. Do you think that gentleness is a contradiction or a confirmation of courage? Explain.

"But let it be the hidden person of the heart, with the imperishable quality of a gentle and quiet spirit, which is precious in the sight of God" (1 Pet. 3:4).

45. Gentleness is tenderness. How do you think the tenderness of a gentle and quiet heart will influence . . .

   our tongues?

"Meekness and gentleness are not opposites of courage; it takes courage to be meek and gentle in an evil world."[4]
—John W. Sanderson

our eyes?

our hands?

our personalities?

Jerry Bridges asks, "Are we dogmatic and opinionated, blunt and abrupt? Do we seek to intimidate or dominate others by the sheer force of our personality? Do people feel ill at ease in our presence because they think we are silently judging their weaknesses and correcting their faults? We need to identify specific instances in which we fall short. Only then will we be driven to pray fervently for the grace of gentleness."[5]

46. While the world may turn a cold shoulder to the virtue of gentleness, what significance does God place on it? (1 Pet. 3:4).

47. How is gentleness encouraged in the following verses?

Ephesians 4:1-2

Titus 3:1-2

48. Why will the fruit of gentleness in your relationships make yours a unique friendship to those who know you?

[1] Jerry Bridges, *The Practice of Godliness* (Colorado Springs: NavPress, 1983), 220.
[2] *Improving Your Serve*, Charles R. Swindoll, 1981, Nashville, Tennessee. All rights reserved. Used by permission.
[3] Michael Griffiths, *The Example of Jesus* (reproduced by permission of William Neill-Hall Ltd., Cornwall, England), 96-97. Used by permission.
[4] John W. Sanderson, *The Fruit of the Spirit* (Phillipsburg, New Jersey: Presbyterian and Reformed Publishing Company, 1984, 1985), 125. Used by permission.
[5] Jerry Bridges, *The Practice of Godliness*, 228.

WEEK 27
MERCY AND FORGIVENESS

DAY 1

1. From memory, write the verse you memorized on "who you are in Christ."

Read Colossians 3:12-13 and Ephesians 4:32.

2. How do Paul's words in the first half of verse 12 remind the Colossians of who they are?

3. In Colossians 3:12b, what issues of Christlikeness does Paul encourage them to pursue?

4. According to the following verses, why should we also see forgiveness as a dimension of Christlikeness?

   Colossians 3:13

   Ephesians 4:32

5. How do you think your understanding of God's forgiveness toward you will impact your own forgiveness toward others?

6. Colossians 3:13—"Whoever has a complaint against anyone . . ." If a complaint against someone is given time to fester, what might become of it?

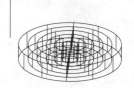

SCRIPTURE MEMORY
Mercy and Forgiveness
■ Matthew 6:14-15
■ Luke 17:3-4
■ Colossians 3:13

Both of these passages refer to forgiveness within the body of Christ. This means that more than likely we are going to fail each other; after all, we are sinners. Not that we are to expect failure from each other, but we do need to be ready to forgive at all times. When we think about the things that are a part of our relationships on a daily basis, it shouldn't seem odd that forgiveness would be among them. Jesus went so far as to say it like this:

"If your brother . . . sins against you seven times a day, and returns to you seven times saying, "I repent," forgive him" (Luke 17:3-4).

We will look at this passage again later on in this study.

7. Matthew 6:14-15—What is the significance of forgiveness in our relationship with God?

8. How do you know when forgiveness has taken place in your life? (Check one)
_____ When you have better feelings toward the offender
_____ When you have forgotten what the offender did to you
_____ When you have torn up the "IOU," so to speak

Explain why you checked this one.

In *Forgive and Forget*, Lewis B. Smedes explains that you shouldn't forget what someone did, because then you couldn't forgive. You forgive because you haven't forgotten.[1]

DAY 2

Read Matthew 18:21-35.

9. Verse 24—Ten thousand talents is comparable to ten million dollars today. This is nearly impossible to imagine, let alone to try and repay. Yet, how does this help you to picture your own indebtedness to a perfect, holy, and just God?

10. Verse 25a—How are we also like the slave here?

11. Verse 25b—What did the king in the parable have a right to do with the slave?

12. Verse 26—What did the slave ask and promise the king?

13. Verse 27—Yet, how did the king's response exceed the slave's request?

14. Verse 28—Do the slave's actions resemble one who has been released from an enormous debt or one who still owes an enormous debt? Explain.

We are much like this servant. Not realizing that he was completely forgiven, the servant thought he had to pay the lord a debt—a debt that had been canceled.[2] —David A. Seamands

15. Verse 28—What was owed this slave?

16. Verse 29—How does his fellow slave respond?

17. What happened in these verses?

verse 30

verse 31

"Be merciful, just as your Father is merciful" (Luke 6:36).

18. Matthew 18:32-33—How does the king rebuke the slave?

19. Verse 34—And what becomes of him?

20. Verse 35—How does this warn us about the seriousness of our forgiveness toward others?

21. Compare verses 21-22 with verse 35. Peter wants to make forgiveness an issue of arithmetic, but Jesus says it is an issue of the heart. What do you think is the difference?

DAY 3

Read Luke 17:3-4.

22. " 'Be on your guard.' " This phrase suggests that we take a moment and evaluate a given situation. When we learn that we may have been wronged, why is it particularly important that we take a fair look and not jump to conclusions?

23. " 'If your brother sins, rebuke him.' " What do you think are advantages of going straight to the one who may have wronged you rather than waiting?

24. What do you think are advantages of going straight to the one who may have wronged you rather than going to someone else?

25. " 'And if he repents, forgive him.' " What is the responsibility of the offender and the offended in regard to forgiveness?

God's forgiveness can be received only if the sinner repents (Acts 3:19). In repentance, the sinner recognizes the high cost of sin. For God to forgive without the requirement of repentance would so cheapen the offense that the very character of God would have to change in regard to sin, and thereby make Christ's death worthless. As God the Son, Jesus speaks of our forgiveness of each other in the context of the Father's forgiveness. Therefore, the "offended" experiences forgiveness by his or her willingness to forgive and the "offender" by his or her willingness to repent and seek forgiveness.

26. Think about it. Why is the experience of forgiveness complete only when repentance is involved?

27. Does an unrepentant "offender" leave the "offended" free to retaliate, to hold a grudge, or to become bitter? Explain.

Revenge, anger, and hatred all cause pain to the person feeling them. If you live a life of unforgiveness, you live in continued pain.[3] —Rich Buhler

28. Verse 4—How do you know when forgiveness is given with no spirit of retaliation or bitterness?

We must be careful. It is easy to look at this passage from the perspective of the offended and ask: "Who has offended or hurt me and hasn't repented?" Rather, we would do well to see ourselves from the perspective of the offender: "To whom do I need to go and ask for forgiveness?"

29. This is the question you need to ask yourself: "To whom do I need to go and ask for forgiveness?" As the Lord brings specific people to mind, write their names below.

30. From memory, write the verse you memorized on "humility."

31. Whom do you need to forgive? As the Lord brings specific people to mind, write their names below.

32. What must be your next step in regard to questions 29 and 31?

"But prove yourselves doers of the word, and not merely hearers who delude themselves" (Jas. 1:22).

DAY 4

Today's passage reveals one of the final acts in a long scenario of suspicion, selfish ambition, and hatred. After he killed Goliath, David had won the love of Jonathan, the acceptance of the men of war, and had secured the praise of the people. As a result, King Saul was overcome by jealousy and rage and set out on a series of murderous attempts on David's life. In one of these last efforts to kill David, Saul's madness is overshadowed by David's own mercy, honor, and self-control.

Read 1 Samuel 24:1-22.

33. **Verses 1-2—As king, you would think that Saul would be occupying himself with the duties of government and the welfare of Israel, but with what was he consumed?**

34. **Verses 3-4a—How did David's men interpret an unguarded opportunity?**

35. **Verses 4b—What did David do? Why?**

36. **Verses 5-7—How did the Lord through David's own conscience interpret the opportunity?**

37. **From memory, write the verse you memorized on "gentleness."**

38. **Verse 8—David is aware that Saul is in desperate pursuit of his life, yet how does he continue to honor him?**

39. **Verse 9—David does not know that Saul's jealousy has motivated the attacks on his life. What had he reasoned to be the motive?**

40. **Verse 10—How does David describe his act of mercy, and what does he reveal as the motive for mercy in this instance?**

41. **From memory, write the verse you memorized on "self-control."**

42. **1 Samuel 24:11—What was the evidence of self-control and mercy?**

43. **From memory, write the verse you memorized on "discipline."**

44. **1 Samuel 24:12-15—In whose hand does mercy leave sin? Explain.**

45. What does Saul acknowledge about David in the following verses?

verse 17

verse 18

46. Verse 19—" 'If a man finds his enemy, will he let him go away safely?' " As you reword this question into a statement below, you will have a definition of mercy.

47. Verses 19-20—How does mercy, gentleness, and self-control produce the kind of royalty that even David's enemy had to admit was inevitable?

Compare questions 34 and 36 and think through the following. How do you interpret the "chance" meetings that confront you with an enemy? Is it an opportunity for mercy or retaliation? A glare, a snub, a sigh of disgust: what do your non-verbals communicate? And what about the verbals? Do you use words to slaughter your enemy when his or her back is turned? "He's got it coming to him." "She deserves it." We must not consider what is deserved. Mercy in forgiveness is only possible when it is not deserved.

DAY 5

Read Matthew 7:1-5.

48. What type of actions or attitudes do you think contribute to a judgmental spirit?

49. Verses 1-2—What is the warning here for such a spirit and why?

50. How does a judgmental spirit fail to consider the voice of mercy?

51. Verses 3-5—Describe the humor of this illustration and the seriousness of its principles.

52. Though the "log-impaired" eye may be able to see a speck in a brother's eye, what other qualities might it be unable to see?

53. When the log is removed, how might it affect the person's perspective of the speck?

54. Verse 5, " 'Then you will see clearly to take the speck out of your brother's eye.' " Everyone knows what it feels like to have a small

particle irritating the eye. Sometimes it becomes so painful that we must call on someone else to remove it. Likewise, how do we benefit from one with a discerning eye who can see and call attention to specific sins in our lives?

"'Do not judge lest you be judged. . . .
Then you will see clearly to take the speck out of your brother's eye.'"

55. Look at the above verses. Jesus says clearly, "Do not judge." Yet He also says that when you see clearly you can "take the speck out of your brother's eye." What do you think is the difference between being judgmental and removing specks?

"The current popular notion that judging others is in itself a sin leads to such inappropriate maxims as 'I'm OK and you're OK.' It encourages a conspiracy of moral indifference which says, 'If you never tell me that anything I'm doing is wrong, I'll never tell you that anything you're doing is wrong.' 'Judge not that ye be not judged' has come to mean that if you never call anything sin nobody can ever call you a sinner. . .The dust must indeed be removed, not tolerated or ignored or called by a polite name. But it must be removed by somebody who can see—that is, the humble, the childlike, the pure, the meek. If any of us are inclined to excuse ourselves from the responsibility to judge, pleading that we do not belong in that lovely company, let us not forget that it is those of that company and only those who are of any use in the kingdom, in fact, who will even enter it."[4] —Elisabeth Elliot

---

[1] Lewis B. Smedes, *Forgive and Forget* (New York: Guideposts, 1984), 38-39.
[2] David A. Seamands, *Healing for Damaged Emotions* (Wheaton, Illinois: Victor Books, 1983), 32.
[3] Rich Buhler, *Pain and Pretending* (Nashville: Thomas Nelson Publishers, 1991), 198.
[4] Elisabeth Elliot, *Trusting God in a Twisted World* (Old Tappan, New Jersey: Fleming H. Revell Company, 1989), 71, 73.

WEEK 28
WISDOM

SCRIPTURE MEMORY
Wisdom
■ 1 Kings 3:9
■ Proverbs 1:7
■ James 1:5

DAY 1

Read James 3:13-17.

1. Write what comes to mind as you read each of the following phrases:

A. Words of wisdom

B. Wisdom of old age

C. A wise business transaction

2. Verse 13—Where does the real evidence of wisdom lie?

3. Verse 17—What does such wisdom look like?

"Wisdom is more than knowledge, which is the accumulation of facts . . . it is heavenly discernment. It is knowledge with insight into the heart of things—that knows them as they really are. It involves the knowledge of God and of the intricacies of the human heart. It is much more than knowledge; it is the right application of knowledge in moral and spiritual matters, in meeting baffling situations, and in the complexity of human relationships . . . Knowledge is gained by study, but when the Spirit fills a man, He imparts the wisdom to use and apply that knowledge correctly."[1] —J. Oswald Sanders

4. Which words from verse 17 are most helpful in expanding your idea of what wisdom is? Why?

5. Verses 14 and 16—What motivates the wisdom of the world? (Refer to question 1.)

"'For My people are foolish, they know Me not; they are stupid children, and they have no understanding. They are shrewd to do evil, but to do good they do not know'" (Jere. 4:22).

6. James 3:15—What is the source of the world's wisdom?

7. Verse 16—Why are we wise to refuse the world's wisdom?

8. According to the following verses, what does the world's wisdom "think" of the wisdom that comes from above?

John 8:51-52

John 10:20

Acts 26:24

1 Corinthians 2:14

9. Yet, according to the following verses, how is the world's wisdom seen in the light of God's wisdom?

1 Corinthians 1:19-20

1 Corinthians 1:27

1 Corinthians 3:19-20

DAY 2

Solomon was the son of David. He was the youngest and gentlest of his brothers, and not an obvious choice for king. But he was God's choice. He was like his father in this way, as David was chosen by God over his own older and more distinguished brothers. Today's passage reveals an encounter with God that happened early in Solomon's reign.

Read 1 Kings 3:6-14.

10. Verse 6—What does Solomon acknowledge about his father?

What does he also acknowledge about God?

11. Verse 7—" 'And now, O Lord my God.' " Though Solomon recognized his father's relationship with the Lord, what personal commitment does he reveal with this statement?

12. Verse 7—What does Solomon admit here?

13. Verse 9—What request does he ask of the Lord?

14. Verse 11—What wish list could he have presented to the Lord?

"For wisdom is better than jewels; and all desirable things can not compare with her" (Prov. 8:11).

15. From memory, write the verse you memorized on "motives."

16. 1 Kings 3:8-9—What was Solomon's motive behind his request?

17. What other motives are often behind the desire for wisdom and understanding?

18. Verse 10—What does the Lord's response here reveal about Him?

19. Verses 12-13—How does the Lord answer Solomon's request?

"'So give Thy servant an understanding heart'" (v. 9).
"'I have given you a wise and discerning heart'" (v. 12).

20. How do the above phrases help you understand what wisdom is?

21. How did a confession of weakness lead to greatness? (Refer to questions 12 and 19.)

22. What wisdom did you gain from this?

DAY 3

Read Job 28:1-28.

"'The earth, from it comes food, and underneath it is turned up as fire'" (Job 28:5).

23. According to the following verses, what does the earth possess?

verse 1

verse 2

verse 6

24. **According to the following verses, to what extent has humanity gone to gain the earth's treasures?**

    verse 3

    verse 4

    verse 9

    verse 10

    verse 11

25. **According to the following verses, who is ignorant regarding the value of such treasure?**

    verse 7

    verse 8

26. **Verses 15-19—How does Job describe the value of wisdom in these verses?**

27. **Verse 13a—Who is ignorant regarding the value of such treasure? (Compare with question 25.)**

28. **According to the following verses, what cannot claim wisdom as its own possession?**

    verse 13b

    verse 14

29. **Verses 21-22—How might the eyes of the living benefit from the ears of Death?**

"'God understands the way to wisdom.
And he is the only one who knows where it lives'"[2] (Job 28:23).

30. **Verse 25—How are the wind and the earth's waters a testimony of God's wisdom?**

31. **Verse 26—How are the rain and thunder a testimony of God's wisdom?**

"Then God looked at wisdom and decided its worth. He set wisdom up and tested it'"³ (Job 28:27).

32. **From memory, write the verse you memorized on "wholeheartedness."**

33. **If God has determined that wisdom is of greater value than any earthly treasure, what must be our devotion for obtaining it?**

34. **Verse 28—When will a person claim wisdom and understanding as his or her own possession?**

"The fear of the Lord is the beginning of knowledge; Fools despise wisdom and instruction" (Prov. 1:7).

DAY 4

35. **In the space below, write the deepest desires of your heart at this moment. (Be honest.)**

Read Proverbs 3:13-24.

36. **Verse 13—What does this verse say of the person who puts wisdom at the top of such a list?**

37. **Verse 15b—Why is wisdom unique to anything one might put on such a list?**

38. **Go back to question 35 and write the word "wisdom" somewhere on your list. How does the mere presence of the word impact your outlook of what you included on it?**

39. **Verses 14 and 15a—How does wisdom impact one's outlook on wealth?**

40. **Verses 16-18—How does wisdom impact the overall well-being of life?**

41. **Verse 19—What was the significance of wisdom when time and earth began?**

42. What is something you are getting ready to begin?

Why can you trust God's wisdom as you set out on such a journey? (Refer to question 41.)

43. Verse 21—What does this verse say to indicate that wisdom is not only for the beginning of the journey?

44. Verse 21—"Keep sound wisdom and discretion." What promises become yours as you remain on this path?

verse 22

verse 23

verse 24

DAY 5

"But if any of you lacks wisdom, let him ask of God, who gives to all men generously and without reproach, and it will be given to him" (Jas. 1:5).

45. As you consider the above verse, does wisdom depend on . . . (Circle one)

a. Reason   b. Research   c. Relationship

Explain.

"If you want to learn theology you have to study. If you seek to master any science you have to betake yourself to the appropriate discipline. It is of no use to pray to God to make you a good geologist, or botanist, or lawyer, or doctor, unless you also take the necessary means to become one. But if a man wants the divine wisdom, let him get down on his knees. That is the best place to secure it."[5] —Alexander Maclaren

"We are encouraged to ask for wisdom. God, through the person of the Holy Spirit, is more than willing to give us the wisdom we need for the decisions we face. We are encouraged to ask for wisdom rather than direction. Yet our tendency is just the opposite."[6] —Charles Stanley

46. What do you think is the difference between asking for wisdom and asking for direction?

"God never has to agonize over a decision. He does not even have to deliberate within Himself or consult others outside of Himself. His wisdom is intuitive, infinite, and infallible."[4] —Jerry Bridges

47. "Let him ask of God, who gives to all men generously and without reproach." What does the generous gift of wisdom reveal to you about God?

Read Proverbs 2:2-6.

48. Verse 2—"Make your ear attentive to wisdom." As your ear stands at attention, to what will it be listening? (Refer to verse 6b.)

"But if any of you lacks wisdom, let him ask of God . . . But let him ask in faith, without any doubting" (Jas. 1:5-6).

49. Proverbs 2:2-5—In these verses, what words describe the earnestness of faith when praying for wisdom?

50. Verse 5—How does this verse describe the heart of wisdom?

51. What is an area of your life for which you need the wisdom of God?

52. Will you turn to reason, research, or a relationship? Explain.

"For the Lord gives wisdom" (Prov. 2:6).

[1] J. Oswald Sanders, *Spiritual Leadership* (Chicago: Moody Press, 1967, 1980, 1986), 75. Used by permission.
[2] *The Everyday Bible, New Century Version* (Dallas: Word Publishing, 1987, 1988).
[3] Ibid.
[4] Jerry Bridges, *Trusting God* (Colorado Springs: NavPress, 1988, 1993), 118.
[5] Alexander Maclaren, *Expositions of Holy Scripture: James* (Grand Rapids, Michigan: Baker Book House, 1974, 1977), 363, 364.
[6] Charles Stanley, *The Wonderful Spirit Filled Life* (Nashville: Thomas Nelson, 1992), 222.

WEEK 29
A MORE EXCELLENT WAY

DAY 1

1. How do you know when someone loves you?

2. How do you think your peers would answer this same question?

3. How do you know when you love someone else?

4. In the space below, write a few lines from a recent secular love song. Choose a song which you think emphasizes an aspect of the world's concept of love.

Read John 15:12-13.

5. The Bible never records an instance when Jesus said to someone, "I love you." And yet generations have looked to Him as the example of what love is. When He commands that we love one another, as He has loved us (v. 12), what do you think He means?

6. Verse 13—How does He define the greatest love?

7. Think of a specific example of how Jesus demonstrated the greatest love in the life He lived?

8. How did He demonstrate the greatest love in the death He died?

"The disciples had several opportunities to see Jesus' inner character. They observed His humility as He submitted himself for baptism before John. They looked on as He showed respect for His mother at the wedding reception. They beheld His courage when He confronted the powerful religious leaders and intellectuals of His day. But the most impressive dimension of His identity was that He loved—He loved His Father and He loved people. Jesus was a

SCRIPTURE MEMORY
Love
■ John 15:12-13
■ 1 John 3:14
■ 1 John 3:16

warm man who was willing to spend hours ministering to the 'have-nots,' the down-and-outers, those to whom other religious leaders would not give the time of day."[1] —Bill Hull

9. What contrasts regarding love do you see in the first four questions (1-4) as compared with the next four questions (5-8)?

10. What have you learned about true love today?

DAY 2

Read 1 Corinthians 13:1-13.

11. Verses 1-2—What spiritual gifts are specifically mentioned here?

12. Verses 1-2—What is true of these gifts and the person who possesses them, when love is absent?

13. Verse 3—What spiritual deeds are specifically mentioned here?

14. Verse 3—What is true of these deeds and the person who performs them, when love is absent?

15. From memory, write the verse you memorized on "wholeheartedness."

16. Based on questions 11-14, would you agree or disagree with this statement: "It is not how big the task, but how much love you pour into the task that determines its eternal value"? Explain.

17. In verses 4-8a, Paul characterizes this love in two ways: what love is and what it is not. Under the correct headings below, write the specifics of what he reveals.

What love is/does   **What love isn't/does not**

18. Which inclusion (above) is most surprising to you?

How does this help broaden your understanding of love?

19. Look again at questions 11 and 13. What emphasis is placed on these gifts and deeds in the body of believers today?

20. Verse 8b—Yet, what are the limitations of such gifts?

21. Verse 13—How does this differ from faith, hope, and love?

"But the greatest of these is love" (1 Cor. 13:13).

DAY 3

Read 1 John 4:10-13, 20-21.

22. Verse 10—What does John say love is in this verse and what does he say it is not?

"But God demonstrates His own love toward us, in that while we were yet sinners, Christ died for us" (Rom. 5:8).

23. When you consider the verse above, why is God's love for us such an extraordinary love?

24. Verse 11—How may we share in demonstrating such an extraordinary love?

True love is not really tested in loving a perfect God. We can easily set our affections on Him. The proof that God's love abides in us is when we can love an imperfect sinner. This is when His love was demonstrated to us (Rom. 5:8).

25. Verse 13—How is this made possible?

"Contemplate the love of Christ, and you will love. Stand before that mirror, reflect Christ's character, and you will be changed into the same image from tenderness to tenderness. There is no other way. You cannot love to order. You can only look at the lovely object, and fall in love with it, and grow into likeness to it. . . Put a piece of iron in the presence of a magnetized body, and that piece of iron for a time becomes magnetized. It is charged with an attractive force in the mere presence of the original force, and as long as you leave the two side by side, they are both magnets alike. Remain side by side with Him who loved us, and gave Himself for us, and you too will become a centre of power, a permanently attractive force; and like Him you will draw all men unto you, like Him you will be drawn unto all men. That is the inevitable effect of Love."[2]
—Henry Drummond

"And God created man in His own image, in the image of God He created him; male and female He created them" (Gen. 1:27).

26. 1 John 4:12—"No one has beheld God at any time." Yet, when you consider the above verse, how may we get a glimpse of God?

"And the King will answer and say to them, 'Truly I say to you, to the extent that you did it to one of these brothers of Mine, even the least of them, you did it to Me'" (Matt. 25:40).

27. 1 John 4:20—When you love your brother, who are you actually loving?

    When you hate your brother, who are you actually hating?

28. Why do you think it is impossible to separate your love for God from your love for others?

29. From memory, write the verse you memorized on "temptation."

30. What will help you resist the temptation to hate another person?

"We also ought to love one another" (v. 11).
"The one who loves God should love his brother also" (v. 21).

31. Consider the above principles. We know what we ought to do (v. 11). We know what we should do (v. 21). How has today's study helped you move from "I should" and "I ought" to "I will"?

DAY 4

Read 1 John 3:14-20.

32. Verse 14a—How does the first phrase in this verse describe salvation?

"He who does not love abides in death" (v. 14).

33. Verse 15—What abides with death?

34. Verse 14—When is love the evidence that one has been given salvation and the eternal life that goes with it?

35. Verse 16a—When was love confirmed? (Compare with questions 1 and 3.)

36. Verse 16b—When is our love for another confirmed?

37. Verses 16-18—Is love characterized in this passage as (Circle one)

a sentiment?   an emotion?   an action?

Why can such a love be trusted?

38. Verses 17-18—According to these verses, how can you lay down your life for another?

39. What do you think are other ways you can lay down your life for someone else?

40. From memory, write the verse you memorized on "faithfulness."

41. "But whoever has the world's goods, and beholds his brother in need"—"But I was not aware of anyone in need." Do you think this statement reveals a lack of need or something else? Explain.

42. From memory, write the verse you memorized on "time."

43. Why must we make love a priority, as described in verses 16-18? (See vv. 14,19.)

DAY 5

Read Romans 13:8-10.

44. How does our nation's laws place a person under obligation in regard to . . .

Taxes

Birth certificate

Serving on a jury

Obtaining a social security card

Attending school

45. If the law did not require these of you, would you do/have them?

Have you ever been motivated to exceed any of these requirements: to go to school on Saturdays, to volunteer to serve on a jury?

Explain.

46. Verse 9a—Write the specific requirements of the Mosaic law listed here.

47. What is the difference between carrying out the law from a motive of duty and carrying it out from a motive of love?

"He who loves his neighbor has fulfilled the law" (v. 8).
"Love therefore is the fulfillment of the law" (v. 10).

48. How does love fulfill and even exceed the law?

"It is summed up in this saying,
'You shall love yourneighbor as yourself'" (v. 9)

49. How does love allow a person to walk in another person's shoes, so to speak?

50. From memory, write the verse you memorized on "hating sin."

Loving another person as we love ourselves not only allows us to walk in another person's shoes, but it allows another person to walk in our shoes. C. S. Lewis explains one aspect of this principle like this:

"I remember Christian teachers telling me long ago that I must hate a bad man's actions, but not hate the bad man: or, as they would say, hate the sin but not the sinner.

For a long time I used to think this a silly, straw-splitting distinction: how could you hate what a man did and not hate the man? But years later it occurred to me that there was one man to whom I had been doing this all my life—namely myself. However much I might dislike my own cowardice or conceit or greed, I went on loving myself. There had never been the slightest difficulty about it. In fact the very reason why I hated the things was that I loved the man. Just because I loved myself, I was sorry to find that I was the sort of man who did those things."[3]

51. Verse 8—"Owe nothing to anyone except to love one another." How does love set you free from keeping score with other people?

52. What is a specific way which you can "exceed the law" in your relationship with a brother or sister in Christ and lavish His love on him or her?

[1] Bill Hull, *Jesus Christ, Disciple Maker* (Old Tappan, New Jersey: Fleming H. Revell Company, 1984), 35.
[2] Henry Drummond, *The Greatest Thing in the World* (Public Domain: Collins World), 43-44.
[3] *Mere Christianity* by C. S. Lewis copyright © C. S. Lewis Pte. Ltd. 1942, 1943, 1944, 1952. Extract reprinted by permission.

You will not obey God until you want to

WEEK 30
A CALL TO OBEDIENCE

SCRIPTURE MEMORY
Obedience
- Matthew 7:21
- John 14:21
- 1 John 2:3-4

DAY 1

Read John 14:15,21-24.

1. Each of the following verses contains a phrase which describes what obedience is. Next to each reference, write the phrase.

    verse 15

    verse 21

    verse 23

"You can only learn what obedience is by obeying. It is no use asking questions; for it is through obedience that you come to learn the truth."[1]
—Deitrich Bonhoeffer

2. According to the following verses, what emphasis does Jesus place on obedience in our relationship to Him?

    verse 15

    verse 21

    verse 23

3. From memory, write the verse you memorized on "a love for God's Word."

"'He who has My commandments and keeps them'"
"'He who knows My commands and obeys them'"[2]
"'Every man who knows My commandments and obeys them'"[3]

4. Notice the above translations and paraphrases of verse 21. What must a person do before he or she can obey what God commands?

5. How does this challenge you in regard to . . .

    Bible study

Scripture memory

Hearing the Word proclaimed

6. Why is mere knowledge of the Word without obedience to it of little profit? (Matt. 7:26-27 may help here.)

7. John 14:21, 23—What connections do you see between the person who knows and acts on the commands of the Lord and the level of intimacy experienced in his or her relationship with Him?

8. Verse 15—Others may be convinced of our love for God as they hear our words, as they observe our church attendance, or as they count the number of Christian CD's we own. But when is Jesus convinced that we love Him?

DAY 2

9. From memory, write the verse you memorized on "love."

Last week we discovered that one of the ways we can know for certain that Jesus lives in our hearts is if we have love for other people and not just for the people who are easy to love. And it is not a sentimental, emotional type of love, summed up in words. Rather, it is a love demonstrated in action. God's love was defined in the active, redemptive work of the cross through the shed blood of Jesus and is lavished on sinners: those who don't deserve it.

"But God demonstrates His own love toward us in that while we were yet sinners, Christ died for us" (Rom. 5:8).

Read 1 John 2:3-6.

10. Verse 3—According to this verse, how can you know for certain that Jesus lives in your heart?

11. Verse 4—Why do actions speak louder than words?

12. "And the truth is not in him." How does Galatians 5:19-21 describe an atmosphere that is not ruled by truth?

"They profess to know God, but by their deeds they deny Him, being detestable and disobedient, and worthless for any good deed" (Titus 1:16).

> "It is a pleasing sign of a humble and broken heart when the child of God is willing to obey a command that is not essential for salvation, that is not forced by a selfish fear of condemnation, but is a simple act of love to the Master."[4]
> —Charles H. Spurgeon

13. The last half of Galatians 5:21 and 1 John 2:4 reveal similar warnings. Paraphrase what they are saying to you.

14. Do you think 1 John 2:3-6 teaches that an obedient lifestyle is the evidence of eternal life already obtained or the means by which we acquire it? Explain.

15. From memory, write the verse you memorized on "holiness."

16. What aspects of holiness do you understand in 1 John 2:5?

17. So, what do you think is the significance of obedience in one's pursuit of holiness?

18. From memory, write the verse you memorized on "humility."

19. Check which of the following reveals true humility in obedience.

___ A. "Sometimes I give in to sin; I'm only human. I'm sure God is happy that I obey Him as much as I do, which is more than most people I know."

___ B. "Sometimes I give in to sin and I grieve. I think of what Jesus asks of me and how much I fall short, especially in the small things. My life is His own."

Explain your answer.

20. 1 John 2:6—"To walk in the same manner as He walked." The emphasis here is not on the path where Jesus walked, but in the way that He walked. It relates more to conduct than to course. We have already looked at humility as a part of Jesus' lifestyle, but what are some other words that describe the manner in which He walked? It might help to go back and look at the titles of the sessions we have worked through during this study.

21. Of the descriptions you have just written, which ones remain merely intellectual knowledge for you: things you know you ought to do? Which ones have become a part of your life: things you have actually put into practice? List them under the correct headings below.

Intellectual knowledge   A part of your life

22. What use is intellectual knowledge? (Refer to v. 4.)

23. What does your lifestyle confirm? (Refer to v. 3.)

DAY 3
Read Matthew 7:21-23.

24. Complete the following sentences:

A. Not everyone . . . (verse 21)

B. Many will say . . . (verse 22)

C. I will . . . (verse 23)

25. In verse 21 Jesus says that those who do the will of the Father will enter heaven. Verse 22 records some deeds that would seem to be the will of God, but are rejected by Him. What was the evidence that these actions did not originate from God, and therefore were not the will of God?

26. Why does obedience go beyond saying (v. 21) and doing (v. 22)?

27. Why do you think obedience is the living proof that a person has really trusted Christ as Savior?

"True discipleship is obeying Jesus Christ, learning of Him, following Him and doing what He tells us to do. It is keeping His commandments and carrying out His will. That kind of a person is a Christian—and no other kind."[6]
—A. W. Tozer

28. What do you think is the difference between the obedience that can be worked up in the moment, and obedience that is lived out every day?

29. Why is Jesus not fooled by the "worked-up" kind of obedience?

30. What area in your life are you procrastinating in your obedience to the Lord?

As you consider what you just wrote, what is the difference between delayed obedience and disobedience?

"Too often today we listen to be entertained instead of instructed, to be moved emotionally rather than moved to obedience. We do not take to heart what we hear and apply it in our daily lives."[5]
—Jerry Bridges

"The Lord seldom shows us more than we need for daily obedience. Doing today what he tells us to do opens the way for what he will show us tomorrow."[7]
—Lloyd John Ogilvie

> "God never obeys us. He is pleased with nothing but with our obeying Him, that is, obeying His will. However noble, grand, and indispensable a thing may be, it cannot be substituted for His will. . .
>
> From His view He sees nothing except corruption wherever man's self is present. If acts are performed under the guidance of the Holy Spirit they are good and profitable; but if the same acts are performed by man alone their value is greatly diminished. Consequently the cardinal point is not man's intention nor the nature of the thing, but purely the will of God."

DAY 4

Read Leviticus 10:1-3.

31. Verse 1—Who was Nadab and Abihu?

32. What do the following verses also reveal about them?

Exodus 24:1

Exodus 28:1

33. Leviticus 9 records the specific commands of God regarding the animal sacrifices for sin in behalf of the priests and the people. They were careful to follow through with the Lord's instructions. Look specifically at verses 22-24. How do these verses reveal that their sacrifices were acceptable to the Lord?

34. Leviticus 10:1—What type of offering did Nadab and Abihu present, and what does this verse say about it?

35. Verse 2—What became of them?

36. Verse 3—How had they fallen short of God's command?

Nadab and Abihu did not receive extra credit for taking the initiative. They were not given the benefit of the doubt for good intentions. And theirs was not a sacrifice described as a "creative expression of artistic interpretation." They presumed upon God. In their pride, they thought they could come before Him on their own terms. They thought that anything done in His name would be OK. They were wrong.

How often does our work resemble that of Nadab and Abihu? How often do we rush ahead with our own plans while asking God to bless them, presuming that He is pleased with them? We must stop, repent, and remember that God is holy. It is not enough that we do something for the Lord; we must do it His way or not at all. Sincerity, wholeheartedness, and selflessness are of little use in accomplishing something that the Lord has not inspired. These are only valuable when obedience to Him has preceded them.

37. What do the following verses also reveal about Nadab and Abihu?

Numbers 3:4

1 Chronicles 24:2

38. Nadab and Abihu were probably young, since they had no children. Sometimes the world is rather passive in regard to the evil deeds of adolescence, as though the youthful years were a mere excuse for sin. Yet, as you consider today's passage, is this something God takes into consideration? Explain.

39. When you consider that God had entrusted to them the role of priest, what potential has He created for the years of youth or adolescence?

40. Why is it important that you obey God in every area of your life, even as a youth?

"Let our sons in their youth be as grown-up plants, and our daughters as corner pillars fashioned as for a palace" (Ps. 144:12).

DAY 5

Read Philippians 2:12-13.

"Work out your salvation with fear and trembling" (v. 12).

The fear and trembling that Paul describes here could be compared to what a brain surgeon might experience when he operates on a patient. His fear is not terror. He doesn't tremble because he is scared. He has performed the surgery many times. Rather, his fear is a sense of awe because so much is at stake. This is the sort of awe that we must experience as we work out our salvation, for doing God's work is a gravely serious matter.

41. If we have this kind of fear and trembling in working out our salvation, how will it impact each day that we live?

42. Verse 12—How had the presence of Paul affected the Philippians' obedience in working out their salvation?

43. Verses 12-13—How does Paul encourage them in his absence?

Paul says that for the church of Philippi to obey God because of their love for him was not right. They must obey God because of their love for God.

44. Verse 13—What does he say about God here?

45. Read 1 Kings 8:57-58. What does this verse reveal about God and our desire to obey Him?

It is God who gives us the desire and the ability to do what gives Him pleasure. You will not obey God until you want to. Your feelings may tell you that you should obey. Your intellect may tell you that you should obey. But it is your will that determines whether you will actually obey or not. And left to itself, your will will never want to obey God. This is why working out your salvation with God on a daily basis is so vital to an obedient life. You must spend time with Him.

As you wrap up this study of discipleship, you need to take Paul's challenge to heart. Is your obedience to God based on the relationship you have with your youth leader? Is it based on the weekly meetings with the rest of the students? Or is it based on Christ's love for you? God has given you everything you need. It is not outside of yourself. It is within.

"His divine power has granted to us everything pertaining to life and godliness, through the true knowledge of Him who has called us by His own glory and excellence" (2 Pet. 1:3).

46. From memory, write the verse you memorized on "endurance."

47. Write a prayer to God right now, telling Him why you will obey Him even if everyone you know turns their backs on Him.

[1] Deitrich Bonhoeffer, *The Cost of Discipleship* (New York: Macmillan Publishing Co. Inc., 1963, 1976), 86.

[2] *The Everyday Bible, New Century Version* (Dallas: Word Publishing, 1987, 1988).

[3] J. B. Phillips, *The New Testament in Modern English* (New York: Macmillan Publishing Company, 1958, 1959, 1960, 1972).

[4] Charles H. Spurgeon, *Morning and Evening* (Nashville: Thomas Nelson Publishers, 1994), December 10 entry.

[5] Jerry Bridges, *The Practice of Godliness* (Colorado Springs: NavPress, 1983), 48.

[6] A. W. Tozer, *Faith Beyond Reason* (Camp Hill, Pennsylvania: Christian Publications, 1989), 29-30.

[7] Lloyd John Ogilvie, *Lord of the Impossible* (Nashville: Abingdon Press, 1984), 65. Used by permission.

[8] Watchman Nee, *The Spiritual Man* (New York: Christian Fellowship Publishers, Inc., 1968, 1977), 88.